INSTANT POT ULTIMATE GUIDE

For any new Instant Pot user, if you are experiencing Instant Pot Problems you will learn how to fix them.

Rahmouni. K

https://www.outsourcingmyapps.com

INSTANT POT ULTIMATE GUIDE	1
COPYRIGHT	8
INTRODUCTION	10
1. I RECEIVED MY INSTANT POT	11
#2 MY INSTANT POT DOESN'T HAVE A *MANUAL* BUTTON	13
#3 INSTANT POT IS HISSING AND LEAKING	15
#4 TAKING A LONG TIME TO COME TO PRESSURE	17
#5 INSTANT POT HAS SO MANY BUTTONS	19
#6 NOISES	22
#7 LIQUID	23
#8 IF I WANT TO DOUBLE A RECIPE	24
#9 SHOULD I DOUBLE ALL THE INGREDIENTS?	26
#10 PRESSURE AND FLOAT VALVE	28
#11 THE *SLOW COOKER* FUNCTION	29
#12 WHAT RECIPE DO YOU SUGGEST I TRY FIRST?	30
#13 THE PRESSURE RELEASE	30
#14 *HIGH* AND *LOW* PRESSURE	32
#15 WHICH SIZE INSTANT POT SHOULD I BUY?	34
#16 WHAT DID I DO WRONG?	36
#17 RECIPE JOURNAL.	38
#18 WHAT IS A TRIVET?	40
#19 MY OATMEAL STINKS OF POT ROAST!	41
#20 INSTANT POT RECIPES! NPR, QR, NPR 10, IP	43
#21 MY INSTANT POT DOES NOT HAVE AN ADJUST BUTTON.	45
#22 REASONS WHY YOUR INSTANT POT IS NOT SEALING	46
#23 PRESSURE RELEASE	48

#24 SEALING RING 50
#25 SEALING RING IS MISSING/MISPLACED 52
#26 NOT ENOUGH LIQUID IN INSTANT POT. 52
#27 FOOD IS SCORCHED ON THE BOTTOM OF THE INSTANT POT ... 53
#28 SEALING RING HAS EXPANDED TOO MUCH AND WON'T SEAL PROPERLY 55
#29 SEALING RING HAS DEBRIS/FOOD. 56
#30 TOO MUCH WATER HAS EVAPORATED BEFORE PROBLEM WAS FIXED 57
#31 SEALING RING IS DAMAGED OR TORN 58
#32 'TIMER' FUNCTION WAS USED INSTEAD OF 'MANUAL' (OR 'PRESSURE') OR ONE OF THE OTHER COOKING OPTIONS 59
33 THE INSTANT POT LID AREA IS DIRTY 61
THE INSTANT POT 61
#34 THE FLOAT VALVE OR THE ANTI BLOCK SHIELD HAS DEBRIS. 62
#35 FOOD IS FROZEN 63
#36 LARGE QUANTITY OF LIQUID IN INSTANT POT 63
#37 FLOAT VALVE IS UP BUT THE DISPLAY SHOWS 'ON' AND COUNTDOWN TIMER HASN'T BEGUN. 65
#38 POWER CORD IS LOOSE. 67
#39 FOOD IS STUCK ON THE RIM OF THE INSTANT POT INNER POT. 68
#40 THE WRONG SIZE INNER POT WAS USED. 69
#41 THE FLOAT VALVE IS MISSING 70
#42 THE STEAM RELEASE HANDLE IS MISSING 71
#43 THE LID LOCKING PIN IS STUCK 72
#44 THE EXHAUST VALVE IS LOOSE. 73
#45 THE STEAM RELEASE HANDLE IS NOT SEATED PROPERLY. 74

#46 INSTANT POT MANUAL BEGINNER'S QUICK START GUIDE 76

#47 HOW TO DO THE INSTANT POT WATER TEST – A STEP BY STEP INSTRUCTION GUIDE.. 90

#48 INSTANT POT ULTRA BEGINNER'S MANUAL | QUICK START GUIDE 98

#49 INSTANT POT ULTRA ASSEMBLY 107

#49-1- Base Unit and Inner Pot 107
#49-2- Condensation Collector 108
#49-3- Power Cord 108
#49-4- Instant Pot Ultra How-to: 109
Open the Lid 111
#49-5- How to Pressure Release 113
#49-6 How to Quick Release Instant Pot Ultra....................................114
#49-7- HOW to Natural Release (NR) / Natural Pressure Release (NPR) Instant Pot Ultra 115
#49-8- Instant Pot Ultra Initial Test Run / Water Test 116

#50 INSTANT POT BURN MESSAGE 124

#50-1- Common Reasons for Instant Pot *Burn* Message and How to Avoid It 126
#50-2- What to do when you get an Instant Pot burn message 132

#51 INSTANT POT MODELS 135

MY FAVORITE PICKS 136

10 MOST COMMON INSTANT POT MISTAKES 139

1. Forget to Place the Inner Pot Back into Instant Pot before Pouring in Ingredients 139
2. Overfill the Instant Pot 139
3. Use Quick Release for Foamy Food or When It is Overfilled 140

4. Press the Timer Button to Set Cooking Time 141
5. Forget to Turn the Venting Knob to Sealing Position 142
6. Put Instant Pot on the Stovetop and Accidentally Turned the Dial 142
7.1- Cooking Liquid: Too Thick/Not Enough Liquid 143
7.2- Cooking Liquid: Too Much Liquid 144
8. Forget to Put the Sealing Ring Back in the Lid before Cooking 144
9. Use Rice Button for Cooking All Types of Rice 145
10. Use Hot Liquid in a Recipe that Calls for Cold Liquid 145

INSTANT POT FREQUENTLY ASKED QUESTIONS 147

1. What is an Instant Pot? Is it the Same as a Pressure Cooker? 147
2. Instant Pot vs. Slow Cooker? 148
3. Why is Everyone Raving About their Instant Pots? 149
4. Is it Easy to Cook with an Instant Pot? 149
5. Does Instant Pot Really Speed Up the Cooking Process? 150
6. Are there Any Disadvantages with Cooking in Instant Pot? 150
7. Is Instant Pot Safe to Use? 151
8. What is Instant Pot's Working Pressure? 151
9. Can Instant Pot be Used for Pressure Canning? 152
10. Can I Use Instant Pot for Pressure Frying? 152
11. Which Instant Pot Makes Yogurt? 152
12. Which Instant Pot Should I Buy? 153
13. Which Size Should I Buy? 153
14. What Instant Pot Accessories Do I Need? 154
   1. Must Have: Silicone Sealing Ring 154
   2. Sweet & Savory Silicone Sealing Rings 155
   3. Stainless Steel Inner Pot 157
   4. Non-Stick Inner Pot 158
   5. Tempered Glass Lid 159
   6. Silicone Cover 159
   7. Silicone Mitts 160

Instant Pot Inserts **161**
    8. Must Have: 100% Premium Stainless Steel Steamer Basket 161
    9. Must Have: Stainless Steel Steaming Rack Stand (5 inch Diameter) 162
    10. Stackable Stainless Steel Steamer Insert Pans 163
    11. Wide Rim Mesh Basket 164
    12. Silicone Steamer Basket 165
    13. 2 Tiers Bamboo Steamer (8 Inches) 166

For Making Instant Pot Cheesecake **167**
    14. 7 Inch Cheesecake Pan with Removable Bottom 167

For Making Instant Pot Yogurt **167**
    15. Euro Cuisine GY60 Greek Yogurt Maker 167

Instant Pot Starter Kit **169**
    16. Instant Perrrt! Silicone Starter Kit 169

Handling Hot Containers **170**
    17. Hot Dish Retriever Tongs 170

15. What Accessories or Containers Can I Use in Instant Pot? 171
16. I Just Got My Instant Pot. What Should I Do First? 172
17. What is the Water Test? 172
18. I'm Confused With All the Instant Pot Terms and Acronyms. 172
Instants Pot Acronyms **172**
    1.   IP, Instapot, Magic Pot, Pot = Instant Pot 173
    2. Pothead, Potters = Instant Pot users 173
    3. PC = Pressure Cooker 173
    4. EPC = Electric Pressure Cooker 173
    5. HP = High Pressure 173
    6. LP = Low Pressure 173
    7. NR, NPR = Natural Release or Natural Pressure Release 173

    8. QR, QPR = Quick Release or Quick Pressure Release 174
    9. HA = High Altitude.. 174
    10. PIP = Pot in Pot or Pan in Pot 176
    11. 5-5-5 = High Pressure 5 minutes, Natural Release 5 minutes, Ice Bath 5 minutes 176

INSTANT POT TERMINOLOGY 177
    1. Instant Pot LUX, DUO, DUO plus, Ultra, Smart 177
    2. Exterior Pot / Exterior Housing / Cooker Base 178
    3. Inner Pot / Insert / Liner / Stainless Steel Inner Pot 178
    4. Instant Pot Lid... 179
    5. Instant Pot Seal / Ring / Sealing Ring / Gasket 179
    6. Knob / Venting Knob / Steam Release Valve / Pressure Release Handle... 180
    7. Valve / Floating Valve / Pin / Metal Pin 181
    8. Sealing Position / Venting Position 182
    9. Shield / Anti-Block Shield.. 182
    10. Condensation Collector.. 183
    11. Trivet / Rack / Steamer Basket / Steamer Rack 184
    12. Water Test / Initial Test Run 184

THANK YOU 186

COPYRIGHT

Instant Pot Ultimate Guide Copyright © 2018 by Rahmouni. k. All Rights Reserved. This guide may not be reproduced or transmitted in any form without the written permission of the publisher. Every effort has been made to make this guide as complete and accurate as possible. Although the author and publisher have prepared this guide with the greatest of care, and have made every effort to ensure the accuracy, we assume no responsibility or liability for errors, inaccuracies or omissions. Before you begin, check with the appropriate authorities to insure compliance with all laws and regulations. Every effort has been made to make this guide as complete and accurate as possible. Also, this report contains information on INSTANT POT PRESSURE COOKER and technology only up to the publishing date. Therefore, this report should be used as a guide – not as the ultimate source of Internet marketing information. The purpose of this guide is to educate. The author and publisher does not warrant that the information contained in this report is fully complete and shall not be responsible for any errors or omissions. The author and publisher shall have neither liability nor responsibility to any person or entity with respect to any loss or damage caused or alleged to be caused directly or indirectly by this guide.

INTRODUCTION

When I first got my Instant Pot, I knew nothing about electric pressure cookers. I was familiar with pressure cooking since I'd been using a stove top pressure cooker for years!

But the Instant Pot is different: it has so much functionality and all those buttons. To be honest, it was a bit intimidating!

I had lots of questions at the beginning and I found the answers through trial and error, or by asking questions on forums and blogs. I got some great information.

These days the tables are turned, and I get similar questions from new Instant Pot users. Here are some Instant Pot tips and FAQs that might help you whether you're a brand new Instant Pot owner or if you're still getting familiar with your Instant Pot.

1. I RECEIVED MY INSTANT POT

Months ago, but it's still in the box it's intimidating me and I worry about the safety! Can you help me get started? The Instant Pot has so many built-in safety mechanisms that you don't need to worry.

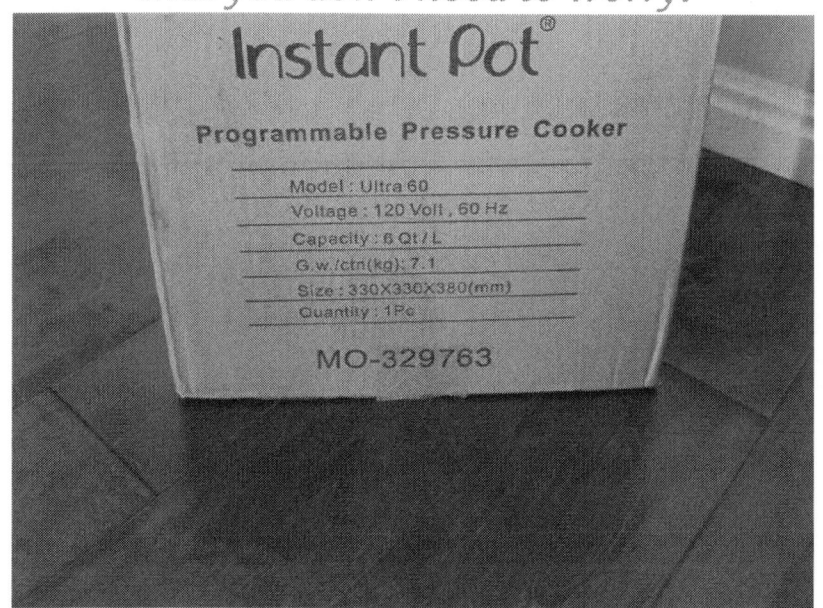

Even if you forget to put in liquid, the Instant Pot will just shut off and give you an error code!

It's very natural to feel apprehensive about using your Instant Pot for the first time. If you're not inclined to read the manual that came with your Instant Pot, I've written a couple of easy-to-follow guides for new users.

It'll get you comfortable with using the Instant Pot for the first time. It shows you the basics, and will walk you through the water test, which is the first thing you should do

#2 MY INSTANT POT DOESN'T HAVE A *MANUAL* BUTTON

2. I keep seeing recipes that say to press **Manual**. *My Instant Pot doesn't have a* **Manual** *button!*

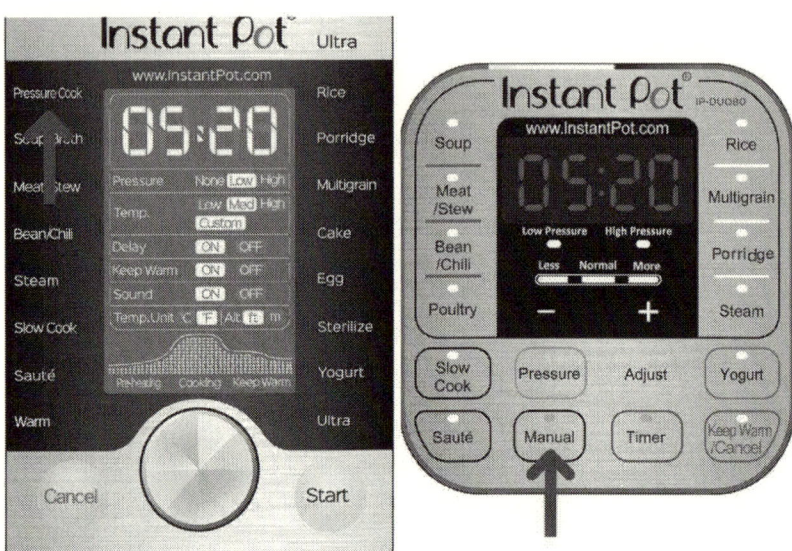

Many Instant Pot recipes mention the *Manual* button. The *Manual* button is replaced by the *Pressure Cook* button or setting on newer models of the Instant Pot.

#3 INSTANT POT IS HISSING AND LEAKING

3. My Instant Pot is hissing and leaking steam when it's coming to pressure. Is this normal?

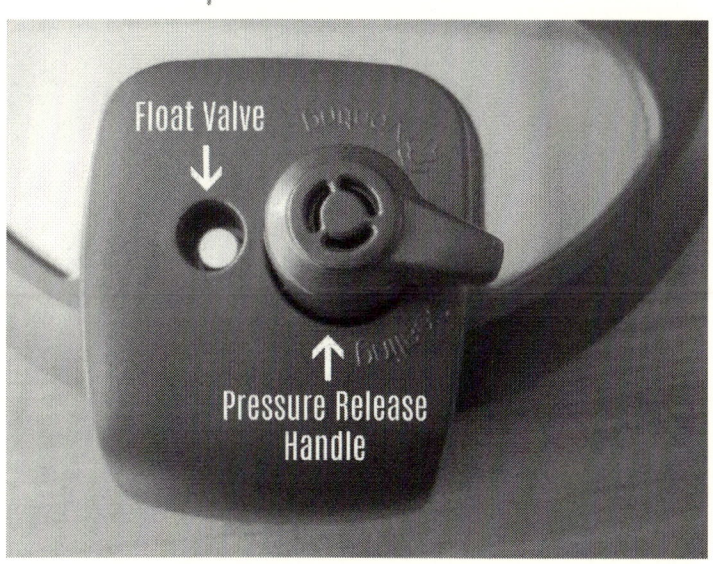

While the Instant Pot is coming to pressure, it may make some hissing sounds and you may see some steam coming out of the pressure release (steam release) handle or float valve.

So long as you've put the pressure release handle in the *Sealing* position and you have enough liquid in the inner pot, your Instant Pot float valve will rise up in due course and your Instant Pot will be pressurized.

Just be patient. The more liquid you have or the colder the ingredients in the Instant Pot (e.g. frozen meat), the longer it takes to come to pressure.

Once the float valve pops up, you should see little to no steam coming out of either the float valve or the pressure release handle. If you find steam leaking from the sides of the lid (where the sealing ring sits), the sealing ring has probably been installed incorrectly.

    If you still can't find the problem, it's possible you have a defective unit and you might need to contact the Instant Pot Company.

#4 TAKING A LONG TIME TO COME TO PRESSURE

4. Why is my Instant Pot taking a long time to come to pressure? The recipe I'm using says to cook on Manual for 10 minutes, but it's already been 20 minutes and it's not even come to pressure (the float valve is not going up and the Instant Pot is not counting down). Where's the time savings I keep hearing about?

With the Instant Pot, 10 minutes pressure cooking time is not just 10 minutes: it can be 20 to 30 minutes. The time that you enter on the Instant Pot control panel (e.g.

Manual or Pressure Cook for 10 minutes) is not the time it takes to cook the dish.

The Instant Pot needs to come to pressure before the 10-minute countdown begins. Think of it like an oven needing to preheat. The quantity of liquid and temperature of the contents of the Instant Pot will determine the amount of time required for the Instant Pot to build pressure.
After pressure cooking is complete, if the recipe calls for natural pressure release (NPR) that can also take from 5 to 30 minutes, depending on the quantity of liquid in the Instant Pot.

But the great thing about the Instant Pot is that while your food is cooking, you don't have to be right there next to it; you can let the Instant Pot do the cooking while you take care of something else. In my opinion, this is where the time savings comes into play.

101 INSTANT POT ULTIMATE GUIDE

#5 INSTANT POT HAS SO MANY BUTTONS

The Instant Pot has so many buttons! What do they mean, and why do most recipes just use **Manual***?*

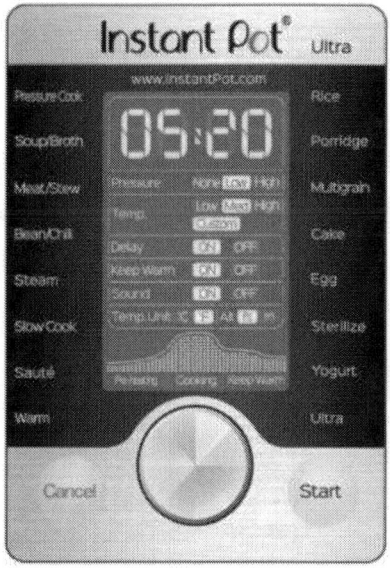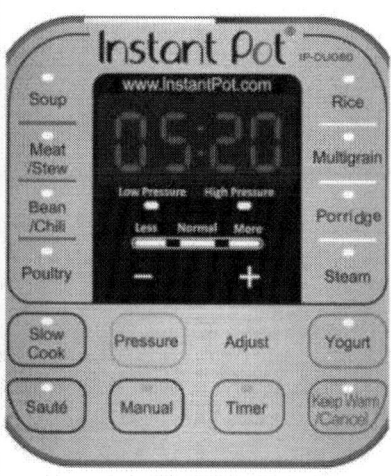

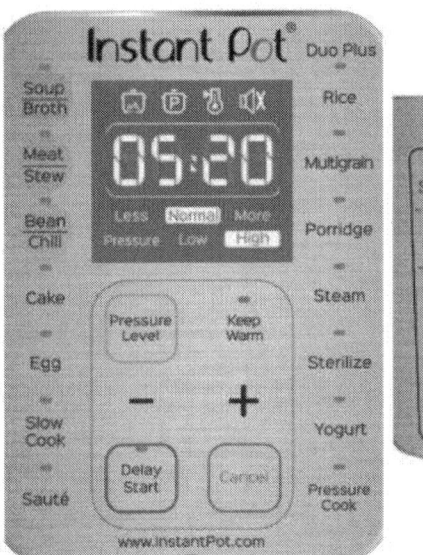

You'll most likely use only a handful of buttons/settings: Sauté, Manual (Pressure Cook on some models), Keep Warm/Cancel and + or -. The Instant Pot has many more buttons/settings like Rice, Meat, Multigrain, etc.

Most of these buttons are just preset buttons (like on your microwave) with recommended cooking times and pressure levels.

They're convenient if you use the same cooking settings every time you cook a particular type of food.

For example, if you cook bone-in chicken thighs every time you make chicken, the Poultry setting might work for you. But if you're cooking diced chicken or boneless thighs, you'd have to adjust the preset cooking times.

You'll find that most of the recipes call for the *Manual* or *Pressure Cook* button to be used. I like to use the *Manual* or *Pressure Cook* setting because I feel I have more control over the times and pressure levels, and because people who own another brand of pressure cooker or multi-cooker can adapt my recipes easily.

* Some buttons (e.g. **Rice** and **Multigrain**) are exceptions: these buttons have some special functionality that is pre-programmed. For example, in the **Multigrain** function, the more setting (or *High* on some models) will soak the grain for 60 minutes before pressure cooking begins. The **Rice** function cooks rice on low pressure.

#6 NOISES

My Instant Pot recently started making clicking noises while it's cooking. Do I need to worry?

There are two reasons for clicking sounds while the Instant Pot is operational. One is that the inner pot is wet on the outside.

Make sure the Instant Pot inner pot is dry before you put it in the Instant Pot unit. The second reason for the clicking sounds is that the Instant Pot is internally regulating power through power switching. This is perfectly normal and you don't need to worry.

#7 LIQUID

What is the minimum amount of liquid I need to have in the Instant Pot?

The Instant Pot requires steam, and therefore liquid, to come to pressure. The official word from the Instant Pot company has been 1 ½ to 2 cups. I usually add a minimum of ½ cup of liquid and that has worked well for me.

I've also found that some ingredients (e.g. some vegetables) release enough liquid that you need to add little to no additional liquid. With experience, and by making recipes again, you'll figure out the right amount of liquid you need to add for each recipe.

#8 IF I WANT TO DOUBLE A RECIPE

If I want to double a recipe, do I need to double the cooking time?

Doubling a recipe doesn't require changing the cooking time. Cooking times are more dependent on the density and thickness of the ingredients rather than the weight.

So, if you're cooking 8 chicken thighs instead of the 4 thighs that a recipe calls for, you won't need to change the cooking time in the recipe (so long as you're not overcrowding the pot and the liquid has room to circulate).
Keep in mind that even though you are not increasing the cooking time, the Instant Pot will take longer to build pressure due to the increased quantity of ingredients.

On the other hand, if your recipe calls for 2-inch thick pieces of meat and you're cooking 3-inch thick pieces, or if you've cut your vegetable into larger pieces than a recipe recommends, you might have to increase the cooking time.

#9 SHOULD I DOUBLE ALL THE INGREDIENTS?

I'd like to double a recipe. Should I double all the ingredients?

Changing the quantity of a recipe is not always straightforward. Some recipes call for ½ cup of liquid, but when you double the recipe, you may not need to double the liquid because that ½ cup is the minimum amount of liquid required to pressure cook the dish.

Doubling the liquid could make the dish less tasty because it's too watery and insipid. So, depending on the recipe, you may not need to add more liquid if there's enough space in the Instant Pot for the liquid to circulate.

Conversely, if you're reducing the quantity, you need to make sure you have the minimum quantity of liquid for the Instant Pot to reach pressure.

For example, if the recipe calls for ½ cup of broth, but you're halving the recipe, don't make the quantity of broth ¼ cup, because your Instant Pot may not come to pressure.

#10 PRESSURE AND FLOAT VALVE

My Instant Pot is not reaching pressure and my float valve is not sealing. How can I troubleshoot this problem?

Two of the most common reasons why your float valve is not popping up: the sealing ring is installed improperly or there isn't enough liquid to bring the Instant Pot to pressure.

There are many more reasons an Instant Pot won't pressurize.

#11 THE *SLOW COOKER* FUNCTION

I am using the **Slow Cooker** *function, but after 8 hours, my dish is still not cooked and the meat is raw! Why is this happening?*

Actually this question didn't come from a reader, it's mine through experience! Needless to say, because my undercooked meat was sitting in the Instant Pot for 8 hours, I had to throw away dinner, and start over.

If you're using the *Slow Cooker* setting, be aware that *Less* (or *Low* on some models) setting is too low to slow cook anything; it's more like the *Warm* setting on a slow cooker or Crock Pot.

#12 WHAT RECIPE DO YOU SUGGEST I TRY FIRST?

I would cook Instant Pot Hard Boiled Eggs or Instant Pot Pot-in-Pot Rice first. After that, some of the easier recipes

Try and choose a dish that has great reviews and

doesn't have a lot of negative comments about sealing problems. Soups are a great option for a first Instant Pot dish because they have plenty of liquid and less chance of burn errors or sealing issues.

#13 THE PRESSURE RELEASE

The pressure release (steam release) handle is wobbly and loose. Is it supposed to be loose?

The pressure release handle is a safety feature that allows pressure to be released manually and yes, it is supposed to be loose.

#14 HIGH AND LOW PRESSURE

How can I switch between High *and* Low *pressure?*

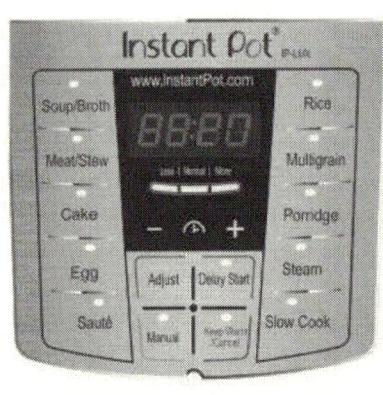

No Low Pressure option

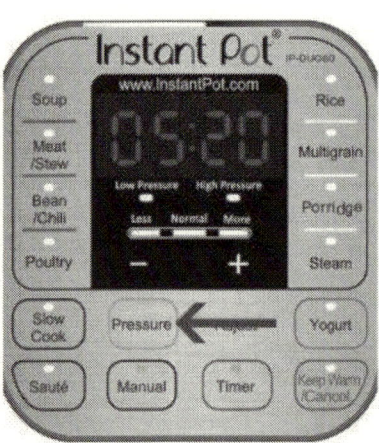

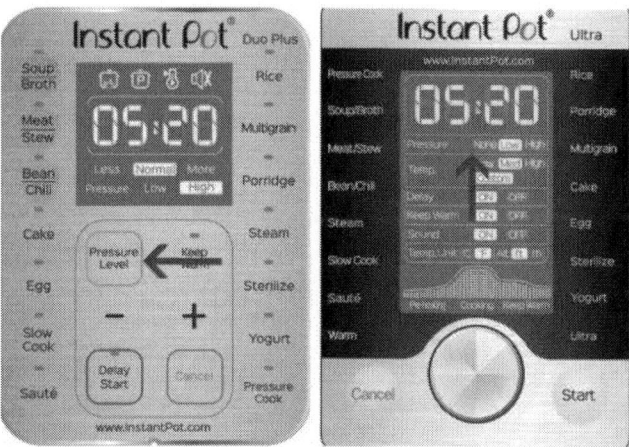

Not all Instant Pots have the *Low* setting. The Instant Pot Lux model only has the *High* pressure setting. For most other models, use either the *Pressure* or *Pressure Level* button to switch between *Low* and *High*.

For the Instant Pot Ultra model, you'll use the knob to change the Pressure setting.

#15 WHICH SIZE INSTANT POT SHOULD I BUY?

Which size Instant Pot should I buy? Should I purchase the 3-quart, 6-quart or 8-quart Instant Pot?

I don't own a 3-quart Instant Pot (Instant Pot Mini), but from what I've heard, it's a great size for one or two people, or for those with limited space, like college students.

I think it would also make a great second Instant Pot, for side dishes. Two Sleevers blog has done a thorough review of the 3-quart Instant Pot Mini.

However, if you're getting ready to buy your first Instant Pot and you're cooking for a family, the 6-quart or 8-quart would be the better option. If you think you'll be cooking for guests and/or you like to have leftovers, I would recommend the 8-quart Instant Pot.

I own a 6-quart Instant Pot and it works great from my family of 5. However, sometimes I like to double my recipes and don't want to overcrowd the pot and could really use an 8-quart Instant Pot.

#16 WHAT DID I DO WRONG?

I cooked boneless, skinless chicken breasts for 10 minutes using natural pressure release (NPR). They came out dry and rubbery. What did I do wrong?

The Instant Pot is particularly good at cooking tough, cheaper cuts of beef and pork, and chicken legs or thighs. Lean meats like chicken breasts, pork tenderloin, or beef sirloin don't fare as well in the Instant Pot.

Meats that are roasted in the oven or simmered on the stove top for hours can be cooked in a fraction of the time in the Instant Pot, usually within an hour, and come out tender and juicy.

I try to use chicken thighs (bone-in or boneless) and drumsticks for my recipes. They are just more flavorful and come out amazingly tender and tasty in the Instant Pot. The only time I use chicken breasts is if I dice them up for a soup or curry – they turn out fine.

If you really want to cook whole (unfrozen) boneless skinless chicken breasts, try to cook them in chicken broth instead of water for 8 minutes. I let them rest before cutting; they can easily dry out and overcook.

#17 RECIPE JOURNAL.

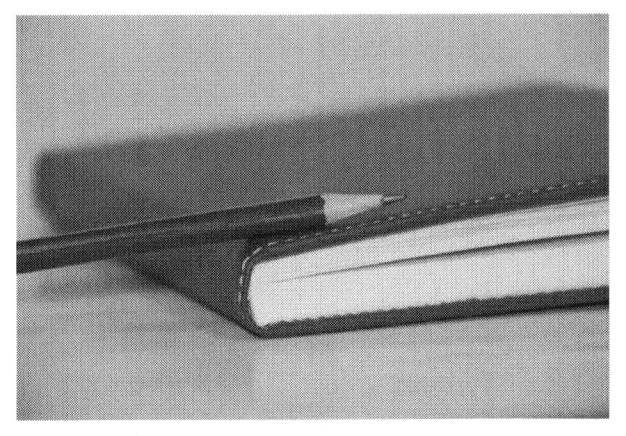

Keep an Instant Pot recipe journal.

Keeping an Instant Pot journal is something I do because I blog, and I always need to refer back to how I actually made a dish, because I'm always experimenting. But I think this tip is something I would recommend for anyone.

Because the Instant Pot requires a completely different way of thinking about cooking, it really helps to take notes and write down what works and doesn't work for you. Instant Pots recipes have to be adapted based on altitude, thickness of food, cut of meat, etc.

It's particularly useful for when you want to convert one of your favorite recipes to the Instant Pot; you can use tips and techniques from your Instant Pot recipe journal. Try it out!

#18 WHAT IS A TRIVET?

A trivet is a rack and usually, this is a reference to the rack that was shipped with the Instant Pot. The trivet is particularly useful when using the Pot-in-Pot technique

#19 MY OATMEAL STINKS OF POT ROAST!

My oatmeal stinks of pot roast! The sealing ring always smells of whatever I cooked last. How do I remove the smell?

The sealing ring is made of silicone. Silicone retains odors, and these odors are hard to remove. I solve this problem by having two sealing rings: one for savory dishes and one for mild dishes and desserts. That being said, I rarely find that the lingering odors in the sealing ring transfer to what I'm cooking.

Some people have different colored sealing rings so they can keep them straight.

Here are some ways to reduce odors in your sealing ring:

- Wash lid and sealing ring in the top rack of the dishwasher.
- Put the sealing ring out in full sun for a few hours.
- Pressure cook water and lemon juice or vinegar for a few minutes and let the pressure release naturally.
- Soak the sealing ring in hot water dissolved with a denture cleaner tablet
-

#20 INSTANT POT RECIPES! NPR, QR, NPR 10, IP

There are so many different terms used in Instant Pot recipes! NPR, QR, NPR 10, IP What do they mean?

Yes, there are a lot of acronyms and you will become familiar with them over time. Here are some common ones:

- **NPR, NR – Natural Pressure Release, Natural Release**. Allow the pressure to go down on its own (float valve drops to the 'down' position; this takes 5 to 30 minutes or longer depending on quantity of liquid in the Instant Pot).
- **QR – Quick Release**. Release the pressure manually by turning the steam release handle to

the 'Venting' position or pressing the steam release button (Ultra model).
- **NPR 10 – Natural Release for 10 minutes (or any number of minutes).** This is a combination of NPR and QR. You allow the pressure release on its own for 10 minutes and then release the remaining pressure manually using the QR method.
- **IP – Instant Pot**
- **PIP – Pot in Pot Cooking.**
-

#21 MY INSTANT POT DOES NOT HAVE AN ADJUST BUTTON.

The recipe I'm using tells me to use the Adjust button. My Instant Pot does not have an Adjust button.

On older models, the Adjust button is used to toggle between Less, Normal and More.
On newer models, pressing the cooking program (e.g. meat, soup, porridge, etc.)
Multiple times allows you to toggle through the Less, Normal and More settings for that program/function.

#22 REASONS WHY YOUR INSTANT POT IS NOT SEALING

Recent Instant Pot users seem to be getting the 'Burn' message more frequently. If you're using an online recipe, it may have been made in an older 6 quart Instant Pot. Because of design changes, your Instant Pot may not work exactly the same way. Here are two steps you can take:

- Add any tomato product and/or starchy ingredients (rice, pasta, etc.) at the end and DON'T stir. Just push down with a large spoon or spatula to submerge in liquid.
- Increase the quantity of liquid called for in the recipe.

One of the most common problems Instant Pot users encounter is that their Instant Pot won't pressurize (or seal). This happens to me and I'm pretty sure it happens to most Instant Pot and pressure cooker users. New Instant Pot users especially have a hard time troubleshooting what's wrong when their Instant Pot is not sealing.

When you first turn on the Instant Pot, the display reads 'On' and after a few minutes (anywhere from 5 minutes to 30 minutes, depending on the quantity and temperature of the food) you'll see and hear steam coming out of the pressure release (steam release) handle and/or float valve. After some hissing and steaming and hesitation, the float valve usually rises all the way up and the Instant Pot is sealed.

If you've waited for longer than usual and the float valve isn't popping up, there's a possibility that your Instant Pot is not going to pressurize. And if the timer begins and the float valve is still down, it's definitely not going to seal. I've put together a list of possible reasons why your Instant Pot is not sealing and won't pressurize.

Note: Once you diagnose the reason your Instant Pot isn't coming to pressure and before you continue with your pressure cooking, make sure you have enough liquid in the Instant Pot. Often times, the liquid has evaporated over a period of time, because either the sealing ring wasn't in place or the pressure release handle was in the venting position.

#23 PRESSURE RELEASE

Pressure release (steam release) handle is in the venting position

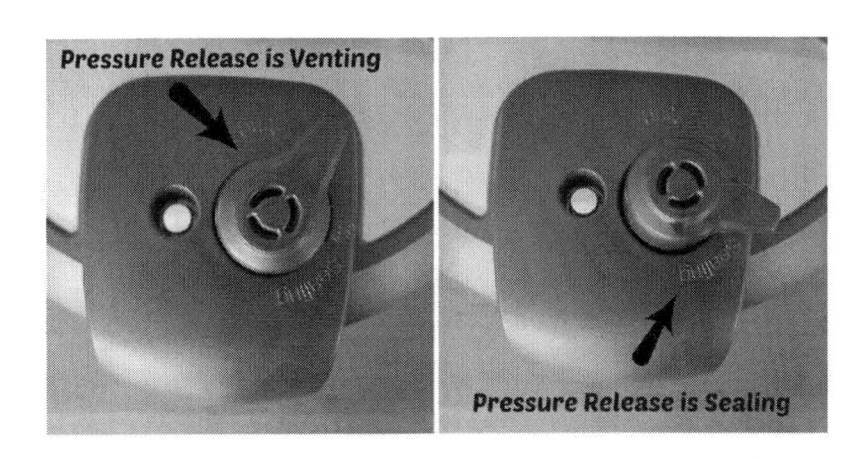

The pressure release handle needs to be in the sealing position when cooking on any mode other than slow cook or yogurt.

Solution: Open the Instant Pot and make sure there's enough liquid. If too much liquid has evaporated, the Instant Pot *won't pressurize. Close the Instant Pot with the steam release handle in the VENTING position. Since the contents are warm, this will allow you to close the pot properly. Once it's closed, move the steam release handle to the SEALING position.*

#24 SEALING RING

Sealing ring (also referred to as the gasket) is not properly seated.

Sealing Ring Not Properly Seated

Sealing Ring Correctly Seated

If your ring cannot be rotated around the sealing ring rack, it's not properly seated. You should be able to turn it in place, with a bit of effort. If your sealing ring hasn't been installed correctly, you may find that steam is leaking out of the sides of the lid.

Solution: Open the Instant Pot and push down the *sealing ring* all around the ring rack to make sure it's properly seated. Try and turn it in the ring rack. It should move/rotate around the ring rack.

#25 SEALING RING IS MISSING/MISPLACED

Often times, the sealing ring has been removed for cleaning and isn't placed back in the Instant Pot lid's ring rack. If your sealing ring is missing, you will see steam leaking from the sides of the lid.

Solution: Replace the *sealing ring*.

#26 NOT

ENOUGH LIQUID IN INSTANT POT.

According to the Instant Pot manual, the Instant Pot requires at least 1 cup of liquid. I've used as little as 1/2 cup and done fine with many recipes. Some liquids like canned tomato sauce are too dense and require thinning out with broth or water.

Solution: Add more water or broth. If the final result is a dish that's too thin/liquidy, you can use the 'Sauté' function and let the liquid reduce and thicken, or you can use a thickener like cornstarch, flour, potato flakes, etc.

#27 FOOD IS SCORCHED ON THE BOTTOM OF THE INSTANT POT.

If food is scorched on the bottom of the Instant Pot, the liquid won't make contact with the bottom of the inner pot and the Instant Pot won't build steam. Here are a few of the reasons food gets scorched on the bottom of the Instant Pot.

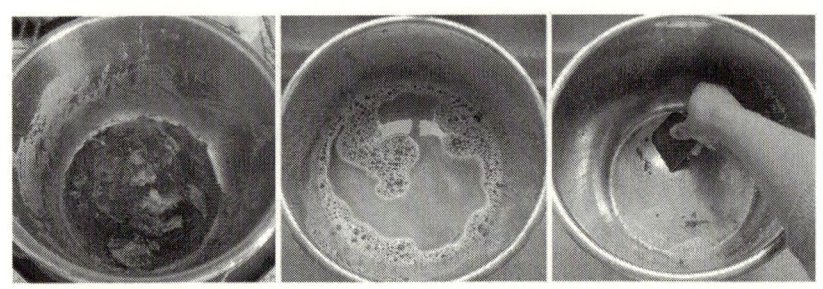

- After browning or sautéing, if there are browned bits sticking to the bottom of the pot, you need to deglaze the pot. Deglazing involves adding liquid (e.g. water, broth) to the heated pot and stirring, to allow the browned bits to come free.
- The liquid is too thick. This can happen with tomato sauce, thick sauces like mole sauce, or thick marinades. Thick sauces should be placed at the top AND you should thin them out with water or broth.
- The Instant Pot is overfilled with food and there isn't enough room for the liquid to circulate.

Solution: Open the Instant Pot, remove contents to a large bowl, clean the inner pot by scraping with a plastic or wooden scraper (You might even need to soak it with warm water and dish detergent for a bit.) I have several of these *pan scrapers* that work really well.

Once the inner pot is clean, resume cooking, but be sure to add more liquid.

#28 SEALING RING HAS EXPANDED TOO MUCH AND WON'T SEAL PROPERLY

The sealing ring naturally expands when it's heated. Once cool, it should return to its natural state. If you've just completed cooking something, the sealing ring may still be in its expanded state and your instant pot will not seal.

Solution: Try placing the sealing ring in the freezer or run it under cold water to contract it. You can also try and turn the sealing ring over and replace it.

#29 SEALING RING HAS DEBRIS/FOOD.

The Instant Pot sealing ring needs to be clean in order to create a proper seal.

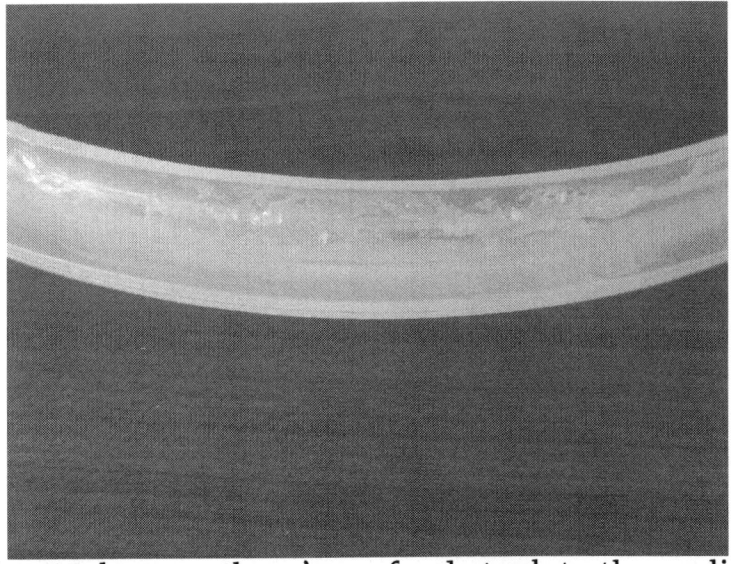

Solution: Make sure there's no food stuck to the sealing ring. Clean the sealing ring with soap and water.

#30 TOO MUCH WATER HAS EVAPORATED BEFORE PROBLEM WAS FIXED.

If the pot was not initially sealed and you corrected the problem, you may have allowed liquid to evaporate and so there isn't enough liquid to create the required pressure. This can cause the Instant Pot to not pressurize.

Solution: Open the Instant Pot, and check the quantity of liquid. You need 1/2 cup to 1 cup of liquid. Add more liquid if necessary

#31 SEALING RING IS DAMAGED OR TORN

If your Instant Pot sealing ring is heavily used or pulled on too hard it can get worn out or tear.

Solution: Purchase a new sealing ring.

#32 'TIMER' FUNCTION WAS USED INSTEAD OF 'MANUAL' (OR 'PRESSURE') OR ONE OF THE OTHER COOKING OPTIONS

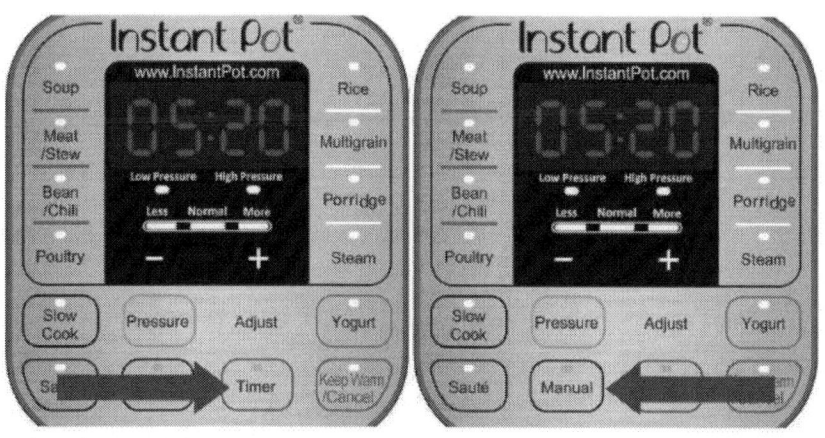

The 'Timer' button allows you to set a delayed time to start cooking. When you press the timer button, the time that shows up is the number of hours till cooking starts.

Solution: Press 'Cancel' to cancel timer. Press 'Manual' or 'Pressure' (or other cooking option e.g. 'Poultry', 'Meat') and wait a few seconds for the Instant Pot display to change to 'On'. If you wish to use the timer functionality, select the cooking function (e.g. 'Manual', 'Pressure', 'Poultry') first, then press 'Timer'.

33 THE INSTANT POT LID AREA IS DIRTY THE INSTANT POT

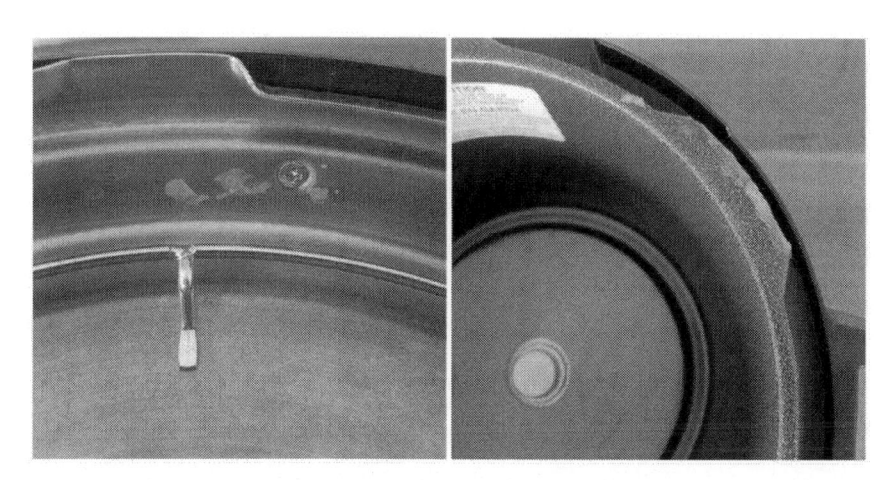

LID AND THE AREA IT FITS ONTO NEED TO BE CLEAN AND CLEAR OF FOOD DEBRIS.

Solution: Open the Instant Pot lid and use a cloth or clean toothbrush to wipe around the rim of the Instant Pot lid and the where the lid would sit.

#34 THE FLOAT VALVE OR THE ANTI BLOCK SHIELD HAS DEBRIS.

When you cook foods like pasta or other messy foods, the anti-block shield and the float valve can get dirty and be obstructed.

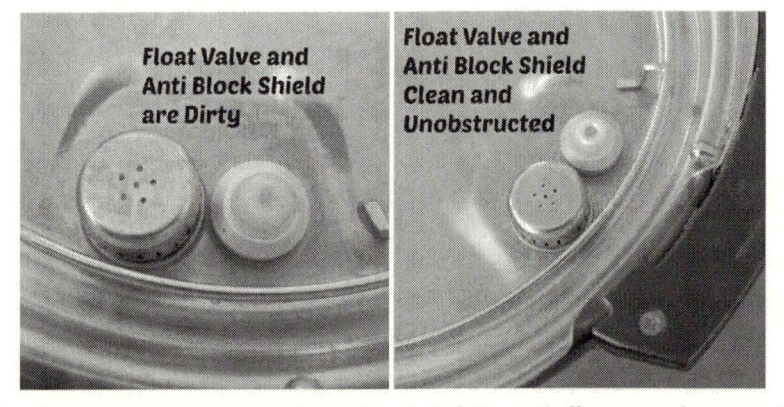

Solution: Remove anti block shield and float valve and clean with a clean toothbrush and soapy water. Clean the hole that the float valve goes into with a brush or pipe cleaner. Clean all parts of the lid. Dry well and replace the parts.

#35 FOOD IS FROZEN

Frozen food takes longer to cook and it also takes longer for the Instant Pot to pressurize.

Solution: Wait a bit longer to see if the Instant Pot will seal.

#36 LARGE QUANTITY OF LIQUID IN INSTANT POT

If you're making a soup or cooking a larger quantity of food in the Instant Pot, you may have a lot of liquid. The more liquid you have, the longer it takes for the Instant Pot to seal.

Solution: Wait a bit longer to see if the Instant Pot will seal.

#37 FLOAT VALVE IS UP BUT THE DISPLAY SHOWS 'ON' AND COUNTDOWN TIMER HASN'T BEGUN.

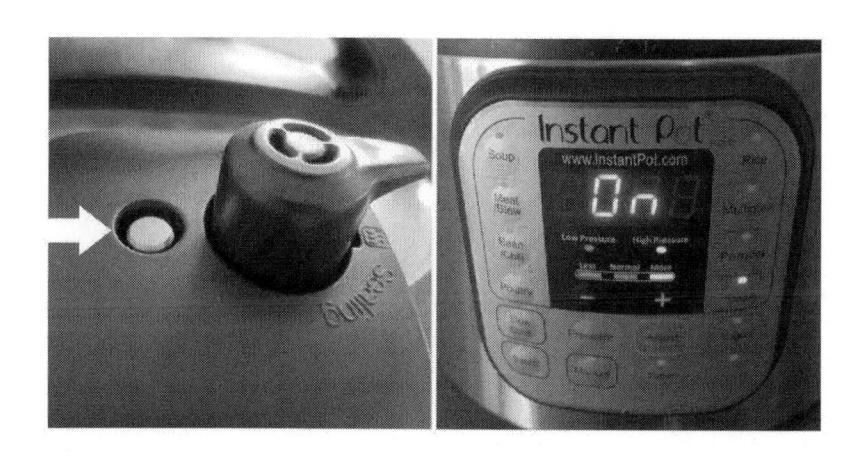

If the Instant Pot just says 'On', it's because there can be a delay between the float valve rising up and the timer starting to countdown.

Solution: Wait a bit to let the timer begin. The float valve coming up locks the lid but the Instant Pot may need more time to pressurize in order for the timer to begin.

#38 POWER CORD IS LOOSE.

The power cord needs to be pushed in all the way. It can come loose if you move the Instant Pot or accidentally bump it.

Solution: Push the power cord in all the way.

#39 FOOD IS STUCK ON THE RIM OF THE INSTANT POT INNER POT.

If you have food stuck to the rim of the Instant Pot inner pot, the seal will not be tight when you close the Instant Pot lid and steam can escape. ***Solution***: Thoroughly clean the Instant Pot inner pot, particularly the rim, inside and out

#40 THE WRONG SIZE INNER POT WAS USED.

If you have multiple Instant Pots of different sizes, you may have used the wrong stainless steel inner pot/liner. This is a common problem!

Solution: Make sure you use the correct inner pot.

#41 THE FLOAT VALVE IS MISSING

If you take the float valve out while cleaning the Instant Pot lid, you may forget to replace it.

Solution: Put the float valve back in and replace the silicone cover.

#42 THE STEAM RELEASE HANDLE IS MISSING

If you take the steam release handle out while cleaning the Instant Pot lid, you may forget to replace it.

Solution: Put the steam release handle back on to the lid and push down to make sure it's properly seated.

#43 THE LID LOCKING PIN IS STUCK

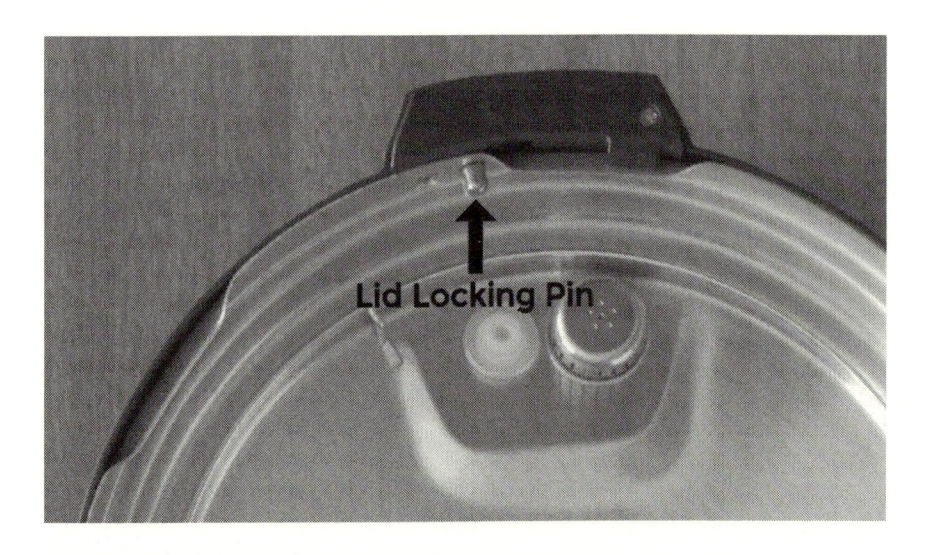

The spring-loaded pin (lid locking pin) on the rim at the back of the lid could be stuck in the retracted position.

Solution: Push on it from the inside and outside of the lid or gently jiggle it to get the spring mechanism to reset the pin.

♦ ♦ ♦

#44 THE EXHAUST VALVE IS LOOSE.

Exhaust Valve

In rare cases, the exhaust valve inside the anti-block shield can become loose; e.g. this can happen during shipping.

Solution: Carefully tighten the valve so it's not loose anymore. ***Don't overly tighten it.***

#45 THE STEAM RELEASE HANDLE IS NOT SEATED PROPERLY.

If you take the steam release handle out while cleaning the Instant Pot lid, it may not be put back in correctly. It needs to be pushed in all the way.

Solution: Push in the Steam Release Handle and move it from 'Sealing' to 'Venting' and back again a few times so it sits properly.

I hope this troubleshooting guide has helped you find out why your Instant Pot is not sealing. Over time and with experience, you should encounter this problem less frequently. If your problem continues, try and do a water test.

#46 INSTANT POT MANUAL BEGINNER'S QUICK START GUIDE

The Instant Pot manual that you wish had come with the Instant Pot. An easy-to-use beginner's guide with lots of step-by-step photos to get you started. This guide shows you all parts of the Instant Pot, how to assemble it and use it (video included). It also walks you through how to do the water test

I just became an Instant Pot convert and I can't believe it took me so long to get one! If you just bought an Instant Pot and are ready to start using it or if you already own one but are too intimidated by it, you've come to the right place. In this easy-to-understand Instant Pot manual, I'm going to give you a quick introduction to the Instant Pot and its parts, and I'll show you how to use the Instant Pot. You know how when you buy a new computer, it comes with a Quick

Start guide? Well, think of this as a Quick Start guide that will get you going and make you comfortable using the Instant Pot.

When I first got my Instant Pot, I have to admit that it was a bit scary! So many buttons, so many features, and the Instant Pot manual that came with it wasn't always that clear. At least to me. So today I'm going to give you an overview of the Instant Pot so that you'll know how to use the Instant Pot for first time without being scared of it! If you're more of a visual person, like me, you might have an easier time following this Instant Pot manual with photographs.   This is the Instant Pot manual you wish had come with your Instant Pot!

Those of you who aren't yet on the Instant Pot bandwagon may ask "What the heck is an Instant Pot?" Well, it's this wonderful new appliance that can be used as a pressure cooker, slow cooker, and rice cooker and much more – the convenience is amazing, I just love it. The Instant Pot that I bought from amazon is the Instant Pot IP-DUO60 7-in-1 Multi-Functional Pressure Cooker. The 7 functions are: Pressure Cooker, Slow Cooker, Rice Cooker, Sauté/Browning, Yogurt Maker, and Steamer & Warmer.

I used to have a stove-top pressure cooker. Oh my, what a difference! No need to babysit the pressure cooker any more. And it's not loud like my old pressure cooker. When I was a kid, my mom's pressure cooker once exploded (!) and there was turmeric-colored dal (lentil soup) all over the ceiling and walls!! I shudder just thinking about it.

No need to worry about such scary things with the Instant Pot. It has lots of safety features including automatically regulating prissiest put the ingredients in it and leave the house and dinners ready when I get home. Rice in 5 minutes, boneless chicken breasts in 10 minutes, bone-in chicken in 15 minutes. You can also set a delay timer and have the cooking start later on. Added bonus – I get so much cabinet space back; got rid of my pressure cooker, slow cooker and rice cooker!

#46-1-Instant Pot Parts

The Instant Pot ships with these parts: base unit, lid, inner pot, condensation collector, power cord, measuring cup, trivet, utensils.

#46-2-Instant Pot Assembly

Instructions

Once you take the Instant Pot out of the box, you'll place the stainless steel inner pot into the base unit.

Next you attach the power cord.

The Condensation Collector is attached to the Instant Pot by sliding it in at the back of the base unit. As far as I can tell, this little doo-hickey is always dry – I've never had any condensation collect in it! *I have had liquid collect in it when there is a lot of condensation on the lid, and I prop the lid open in the lid fin. The condensation drips onto the edges of the lid and drips into the condensation collector*

#46-3-Instant Pot Lid Features

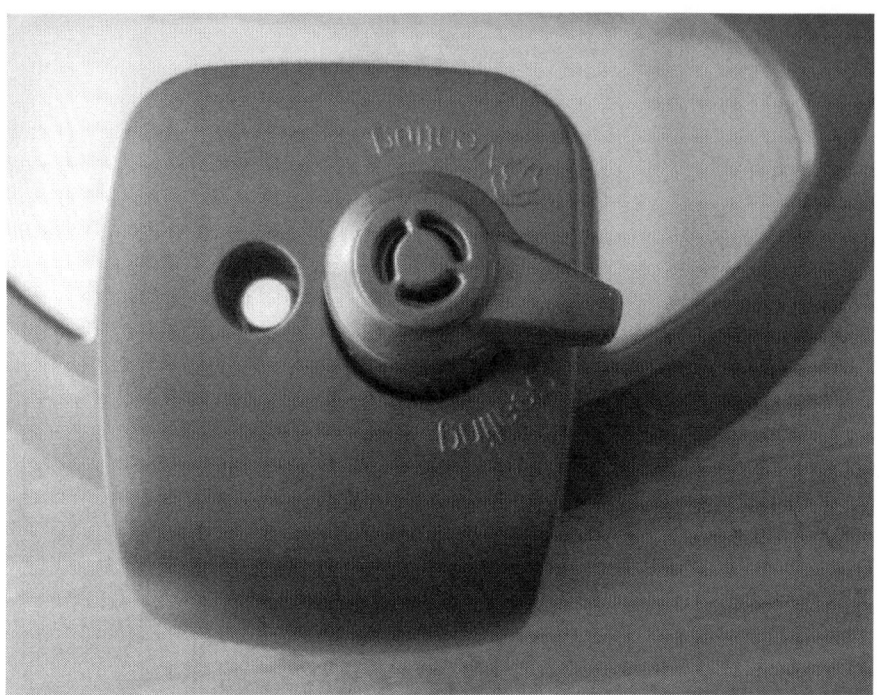

The outside of the lid has a steam release handle. The steam release handle needs to be in the 'Sealing' position unless you're using the slow cooker functionality or you are releasing steam manually, which we'll talk about later on.

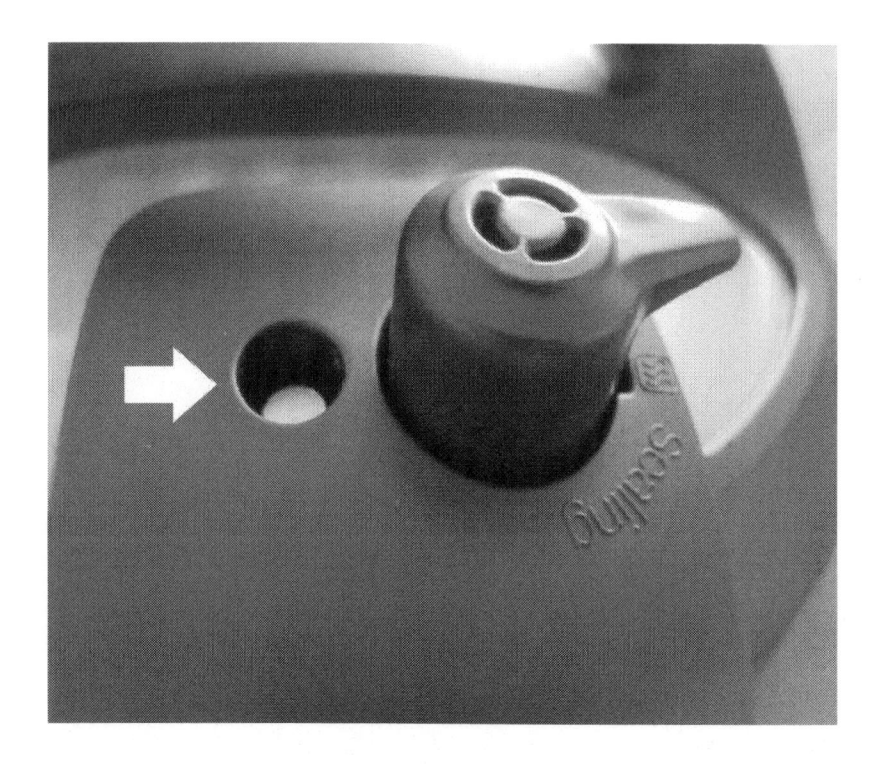

Try and push the float valve up and down from the inside of the lid. The float valve will be in the down position when the Instant Pot is not pressurized. That's how you know it's safe to open the Instant Pot.

And the float valve is in the up position when it is pressurized. This means you cannot open the Instant Pot until the pressure drops.

The inside of the lid has the float valve (on the left) and the anti-block shield (on the right) which protects the exhaust valve.

You'll need to know how to remove the anti-block shield to clean the exhaust valve. I found it hard to remove the anti-block shield with my bare fingers. But when I used a silicone flexible trivet and pushed it with my thumbs, it came off really easily. You could probably use a microfiber towel or a silicone jar opener too.

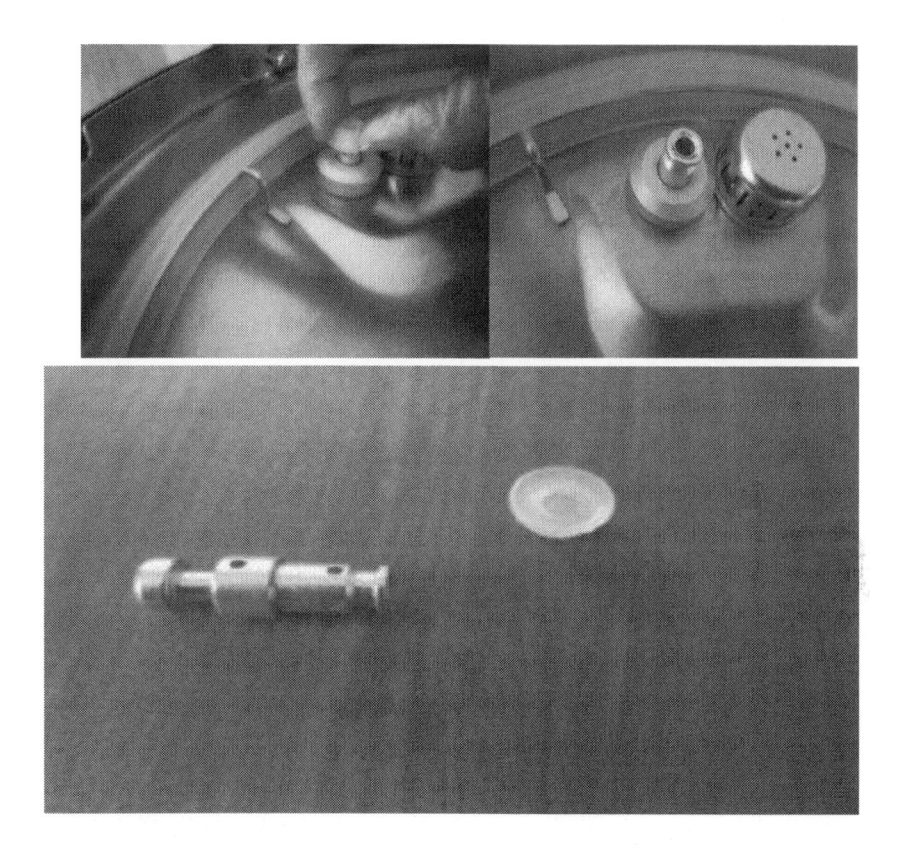

The float valve may also need to be removed to be cleaned. Just take off the silicone cover and remove the float valve. To replace, just put the float valve back in and push the silicone cover back on.

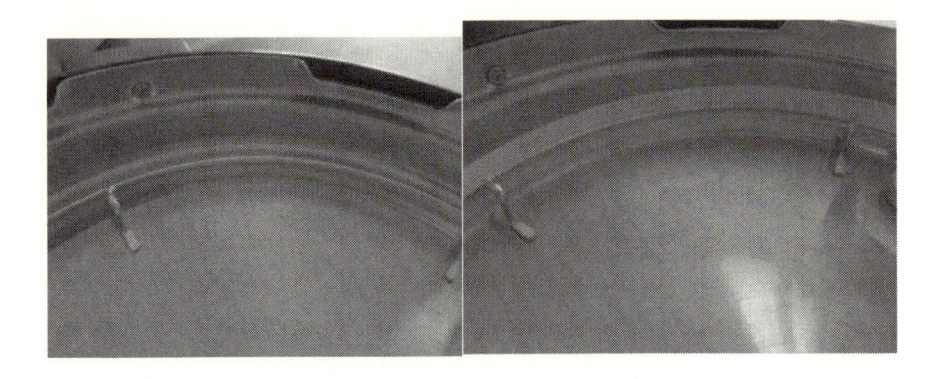

The sealing ring sits in the sealing ring rack and can be removed for cleaning. Don't pull on it with too much force, or it can be stretched. When replacing the sealing ring, make sure it's securely seated in the sealing ring rack. You'll know it's seated properly if you can turn/rotate it, with a bit of effort. If you don't put it back in correctly, the Instant Pot won't seal and your food won't cook. Trust me, I learned the hard way!

To close the Instant Pot, place the lid on the base unit and line up the arrow on the lid with the "Open" (image of an open lock with an arrow) on the base. Turn the lid clockwise until the lid arrow lines up with the "Close" (an image of a closed lock with an arrow) on the base. You'll hear a chime. To open the Instant Pot, turn the lid counter-clockwise until the arrow on the lid lines up with the "Open" arrow on the base. Again, you'll hear a chime.

To keep the lid open, insert the right or left lid fin on the lid into the notch in the handle of the base unit.

#47 HOW TO DO THE INSTANT POT WATER TEST – A STEP BY STEP INSTRUCTION GUIDE

You're now ready to use your Instant Pot! The best way to start out is to do the 'Water Test'. It's just a way to make sure your Instant Pot is not defective and to get you familiar with the controls.

Plug in the Instant Pot and make sure the steam release handle is in the "Sealing" position.

Add Water: Make sure the inner pot is seated in the base unit of the Instant Pot. Pour about 3 cups of water into the inner pot.

Close the Instant Pot: Put the lid on and close it by turning clockwise. You'll hear the chime.

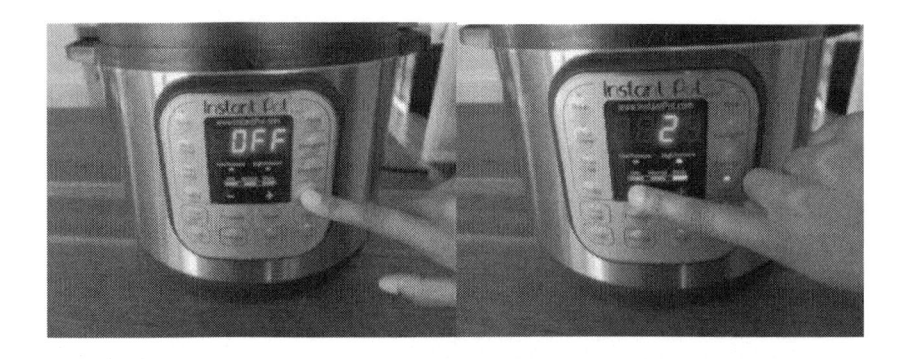

Steam for 2 minutes: Press "Steam" on the control panel and set the time to 2 minutes by pressing the (-) / (+) button till the display reads '2'.

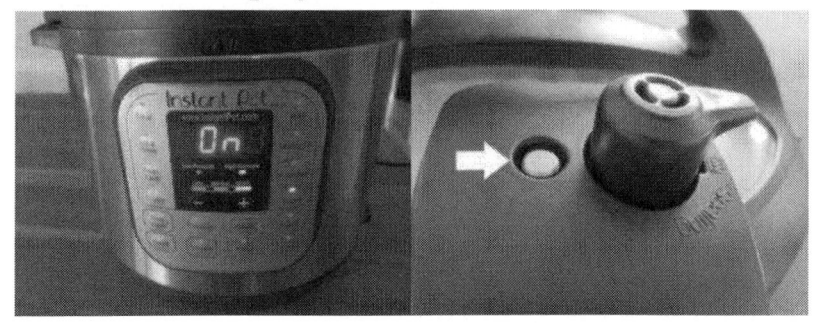

Pressurizing: The display will read "On" until pressure is reached. Once the Instant Pot is pressurized, the float valve will be in the up position and the display will show the time remaining (starting at 2 minutes and counting down). Total time can be about 5 or 6 minutes. You might notice a funny, plastic smell. Don't worry – it should go away and shouldn't happen again.

Cooking complete: Once the 2 minutes have elapsed, the Instant Pot will beep and go into the Keep Warm mode. The display will show "L0:00" which will be a count-up timer telling you how long it has been since it has been in the Keep Warm mode. So if you cooked something and left the house, the Instant Pot will stay on Keep Warm mode for up to 14 hours

In this case, we'll turn off Keep Warm mode, by pressing the Keep Warm/Cancel button to turn the Instant Pot off. The display will read "Off."

The float valve is up, so that means the Instant Pot is pressurized. You won't be able to open it. You can either allow the steam to release naturally (Natural Release) or you can manually release the steam (Quick Release.) For Natural Release, just wait for the float valve to go to the down position on its own. This can take 10 to 30 minutes.

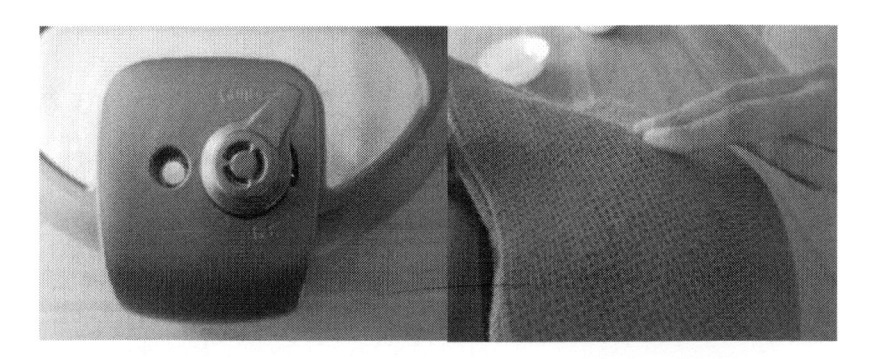

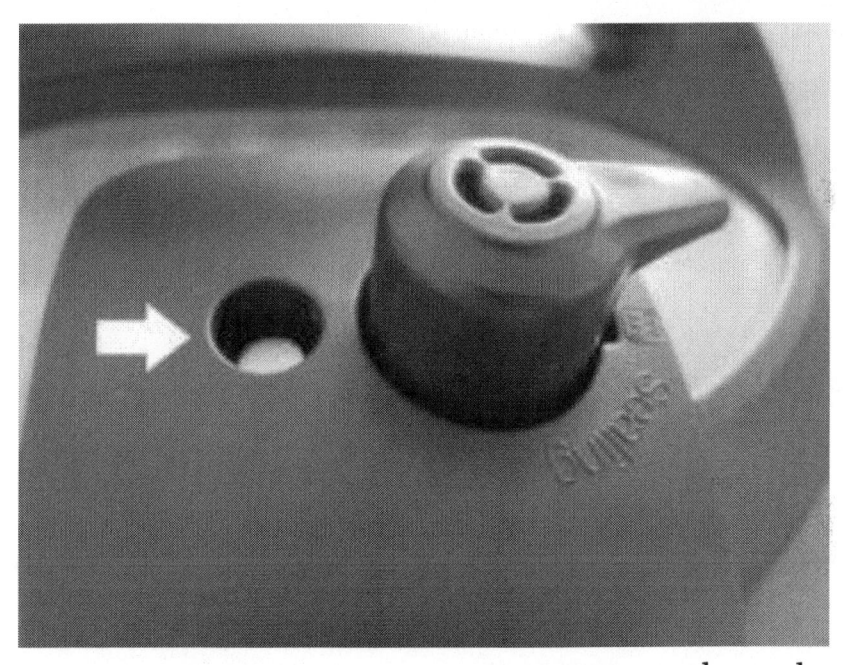

For Quick Release, you need to move the pressure release handle from 'Sealing' to 'Venting' position. The steam can burn you, so be sure to keep your face and hands away from the steam. I like to place a folded towel over the sealing handle and move it to the venting position. Remove the towel once you've turned the handle, so that it doesn't obstruct anything. When your Instant Pot is depressurized, the float valve will be in the down position.

Open the Instant Pot by turning the lid counter-clockwise so the arrow on the lid lines up with the "Open" arrow on the base unit. You'll hear a chime. Lift the lid and tilt it slightly so the water drips into the Instant Pot. Place the lid fin in the lid fin slot to prop the lid open.

There you have it! I think you've figured out how to use your Instant Pot, because you've just cooked your first "dish" in the Instant Pot – water! I hope my version of the Instant Pot manual and Instant Pot instructions were helpful to you.

Tip for you:

Don't try to improvise or wing it with your first recipe. Select a recipe from a trusted Instant Pot or Pressure Cooker cookbook or blog, and follow the recipe as written. If you want to make changes or adjustments, you might want to contact the blogger or ask for advice from an experienced Instant Pot user.

#48 INSTANT POT ULTRA BEGINNER'S MANUAL | QUICK START GUIDE

If you've just received your Instant Pot Ultra, and don't know what to do next, you've come to the right place. I'm going to give you directions on how to use the Ultra for the first time. This instruction guide assumes you have no prior experience with the Instant Pot. We'll go over the parts, important features, how to assemble the Instant Pot Ultra and we'll do the initial test run (what used to be called the 'Water Test').

There are many new/different features on the Instant Pot Ultra but I'm not going to detail them here. For example:

- Instant Pot Ultra has the Ultra setting, which allows for sous vide cooking
- Instant Pot Ultra has the Egg setting, which allows you a quick one-touch way to cook eggs

- Instant Pot Ultra allows you to adjust the cooking settings while cooking is in progress.

I'll give you enough directions to get you started and become comfortable making your first recipe in the Instant Pot Ultra 10-in-1

Note: If you're looking for Instant Pot Ultra recipes or Instant Pot Ultra cookbooks, you'll be happy to know that you don't need any special Ultra recipes or cookbooks – all Instant Pot recipes can be easily made in the Ultra with no changes. The only difference is how to operate the Ultra (what buttons to press, how to natural release pressure, how to quick release pressure, etc.), which you're going to learn here. At the bottom of this article is a *chart* showing you some differences between the Ultra and the Duo models.

I know that many people order the Instant Pot, and then let it sit around for months because they feel intimidated using it. If you've been reluctant to take the Instant Pot Ultra out of its box, know that you're not alone. But don't wait another minute! Open the box and remove the Instant Pot and its parts. We're going to do this together, it'll be a breeze!

#48-1-Instant Pot Ultra Parts

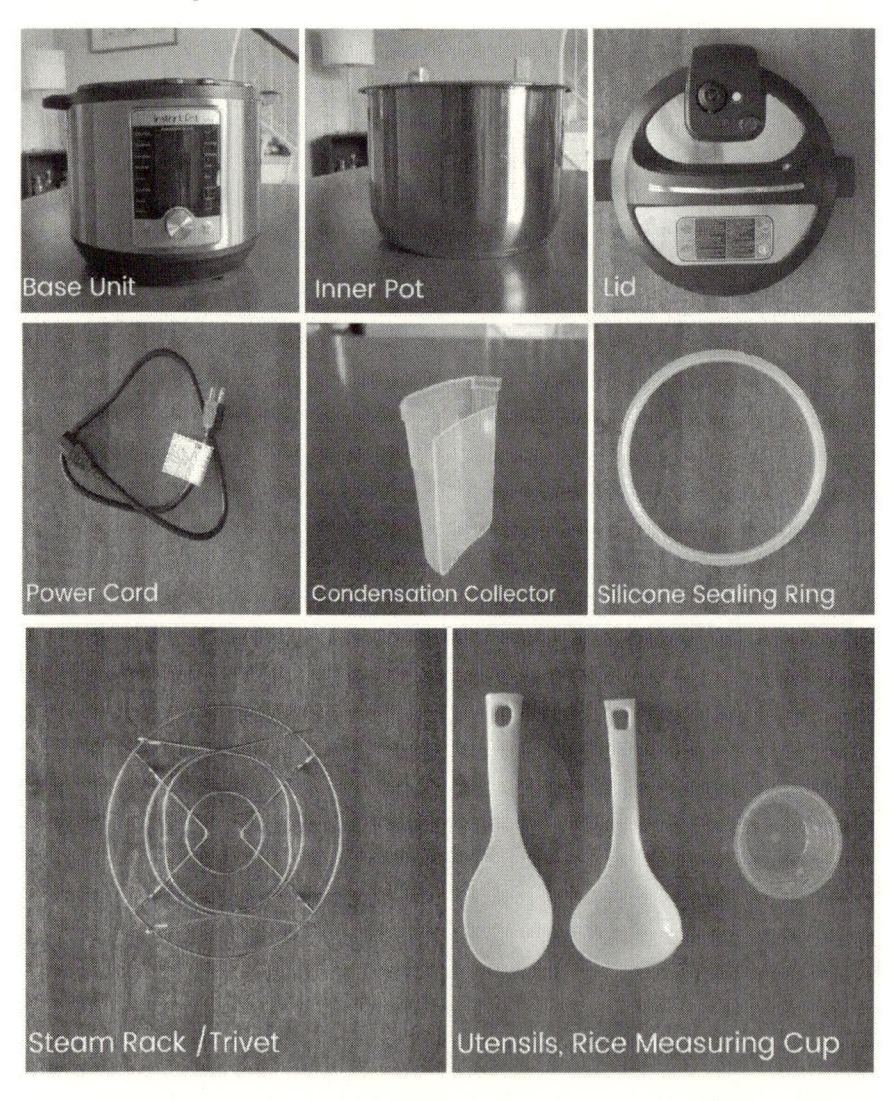

Base Unit	Inner Pot	Lid
Power Cord	Condensation Collector	Silicone Sealing Ring
Steam Rack / Trivet	Utensils, Rice Measuring Cup	

The Instant Pot Ultra comes with the following parts:

- **Base Unit**
- Inner Pot
- **Lid**
- **Power Cord**
- **Condensation Collector**
- Silicone Sealing Ring
- **Steam Rack/Trivet**
- **Utensils**
- **Rice Measuring Cup**

#48-2-Instant Pot Ultra Lid (Exterior)

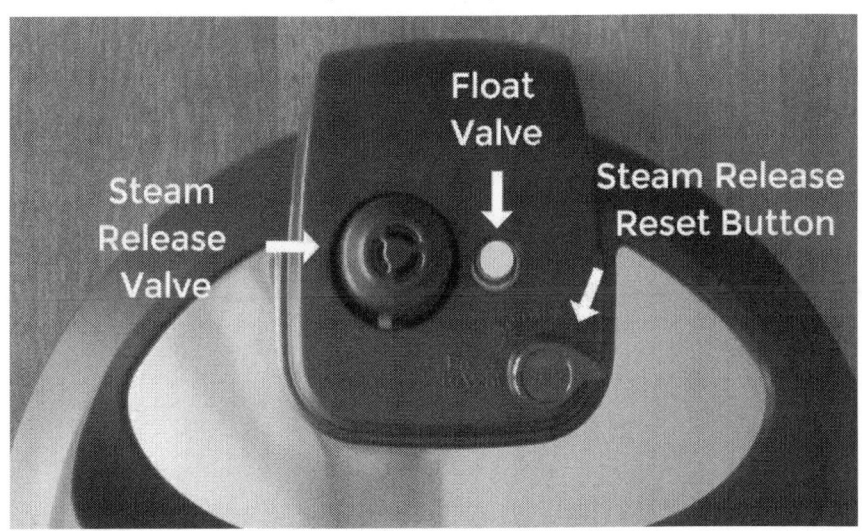

The outside of the Instant Pot lid has these features:

- The **Steam Release Valve** is a safety mechanism that allows steam to escape and maintains the correct pressure level. It sits loosely on the lid and can be removed to be cleaned.
- The **Float Valve** is a safety feature that pops up when the Instant Pot reaches pressure and engages the lid's locking mechanism so the Instant Pot cannot be opened.
- The **Steam Release (Reset) Button** (also referred to as Pressure Release Button) allows you to manually release pressure from the Instant Pot Ultra. Press down to manually release pressure, and turn counter-clockwise to stop pressure release. The Steam Release Reset Button automatically pops up when the Instant Pot Ultra lid is opened or closed.

#48-3-Instant Pot Ultra Lid (Interior)

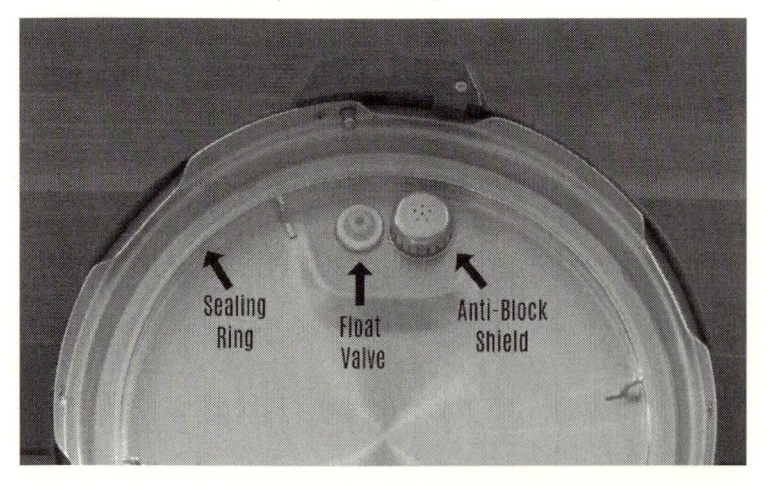

These parts on the inside of the lid need to be thoroughly cleaned occasionally, especially when you cook foamy foods like pasta or rice. So it's good to know how to remove and replace them:

- The **Sealing Ring** is made out of silicone and it tightly seals the lid, and it prevents steam from escaping from the Instant Pot Ultra during cooking, which allows it to reach pressure. The sealing ring can retain odors, so I recommend that you buy a second sealing ring if you're going to be making desserts in the Instant Pot Ultra.
- The **Float Valve** *(as described above in the 'exterior' section)* is a safety feature that pops up when the Instant Pot Ultra reaches pressure. It engages the lid's locking mechanism so the Instant Pot can't be opened.
- The **Anti-Block Shield** prevents food particles from interfering with the Steam Release Valve, especially when cooking foamy foods like pasta or grains.

#48-4-Sealing Ring

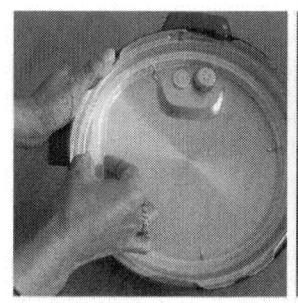

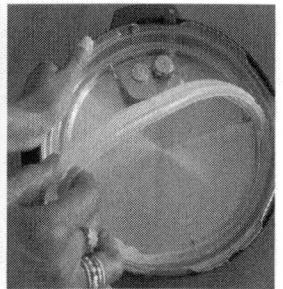

The Sealing Ring sits in the sealing ring rack and can be removed for cleaning. To remove the Sealing Ring:

- Pull up on the Sealing Ring and gently pry it out of sealing ring rack.
- Don't pull on it with too much force, or it can be stretched.

To replace the Sealing Ring:

- Return it back to the sealing ring rack.
- Push it back in, a little at a time until it's securely seated in the sealing ring rack.
- You'll know it's seated properly if you can turn/rotate it in the sealing ring rack, with a bit of effort. If you don't put it back in correctly, the Instant Pot won't seal and your food won't cook.

#48-4-Float Valve

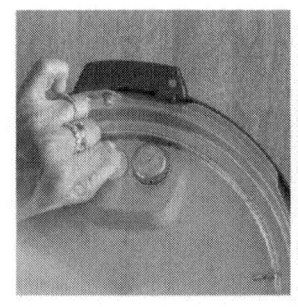

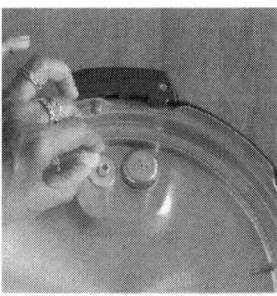

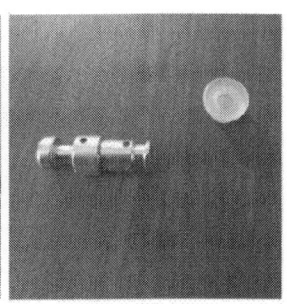

To remove the Float Valve:

- Pull up on the silicone cover of the Float Valve.
- Both parts of the Float Valve (metal part and silicone cover) can be removed.

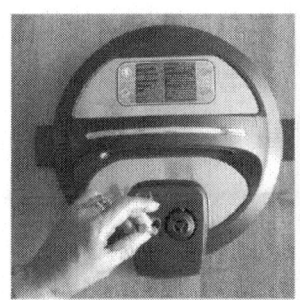

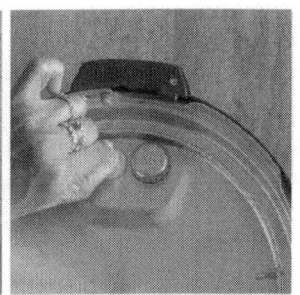

To replace the Float Valve:

- Re-insert the metal part of the Float Valve back into the slot from the outside of the lid.

- While holding the metal part in place, replace the silicone cover on the inside of the lid.

#48-5- Anti-Block Shield

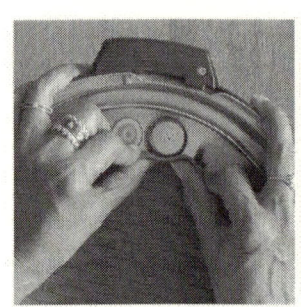

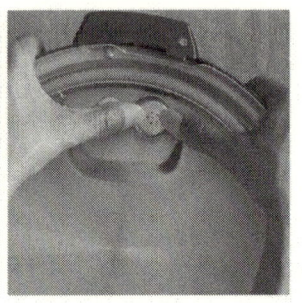

To remove the Anti-Block Shield:

- Removing the cover of the Anti-Block Shield can be tricky. Using a silicone/rubber trivet or jar opener makes it much easier.
- Push against the Anti-Block Shield in an upward motion.
- To replace, push the cover back on.

#49 INSTANT POT ULTRA ASSEMBLY

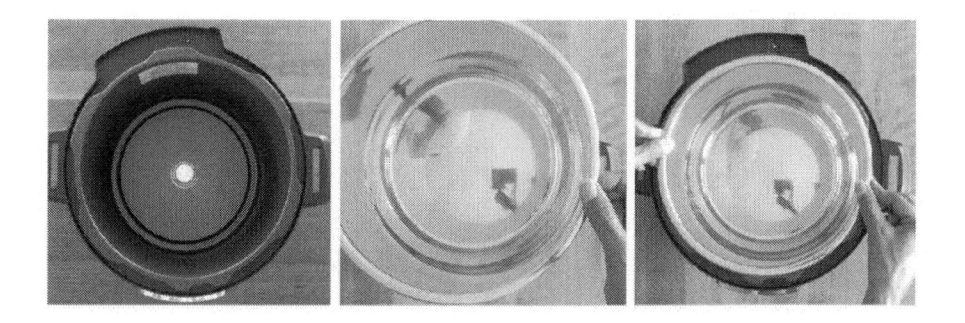

#49-1- BASE UNIT AND INNER POT

Place the stainless steel inner pot into the base unit.

#49-2- CONDENSATION COLLECTOR

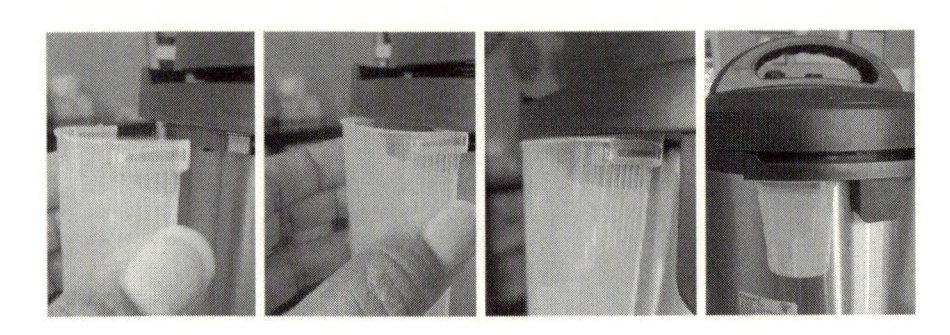

- Slide the condensation collector into the back of the Instant Pot Ultra.
- It will sit snugly against the base unit.
- Although it doesn't fill up very often, it will collect the condensation that drips down from the lid, if you prop the lid open. To clean it: slide it out, empty, rinse and slide back in place.

#49-3- POWER CORD

- Insert the power cord into the back of the Instant Pot and plug the power cord into an electrical outlet.
- The display will turn on.

#49-4- INSTANT POT ULTRA HOW-TO:

Close the Lid

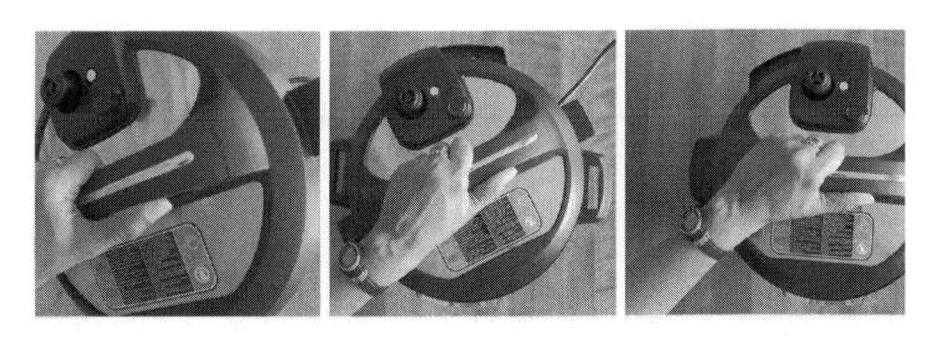

- To close the lid, place the lid on the Instant Pot base unit and line up the arrow on the lid with the

"Open" (image of an open lock with an arrow) on the base unit.
- Turn the lid clockwise until the lid arrow lines up with the "Close" (an image of a closed lock with an arrow) on the base. You'll hear a chime (if the Instant Pot Ultra is plugged in).

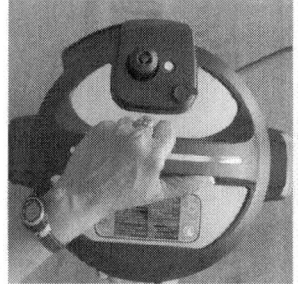

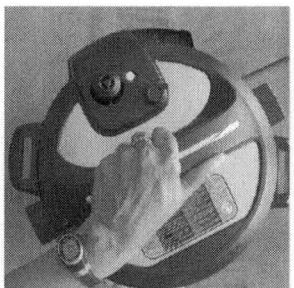

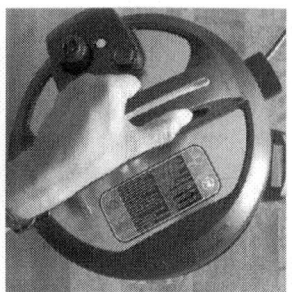

OPEN THE LID

- To open the lid, turn the lid counter-clockwise until the lid arrow lines up with the "Open" (an image of an open lock with an arrow) on the base.
- You'll hear a chime (if the Instant Pot Ultra is plugged in). This feature can be turned off

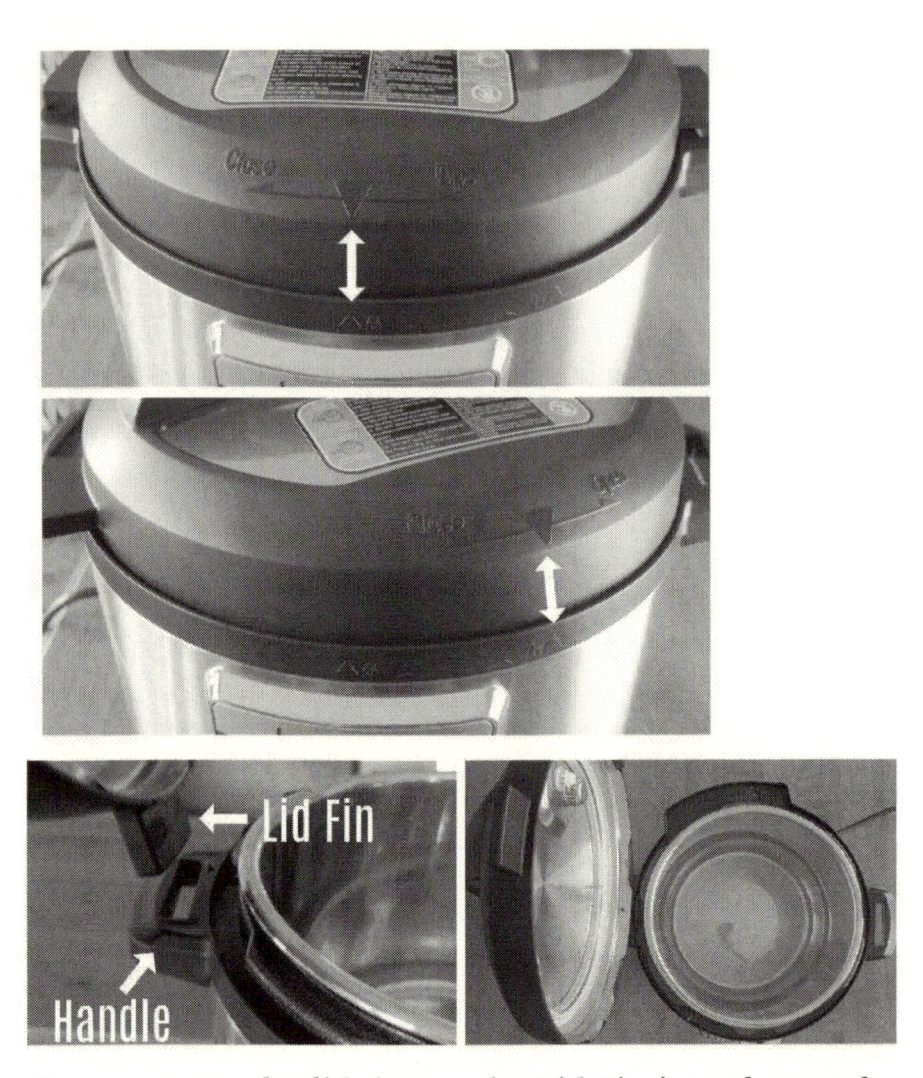

To prop open the lid, insert the Lid Fin into the notch in the handle of the Instant Pot Ultra.

#49-5- HOW TO PRESSURE RELEASE

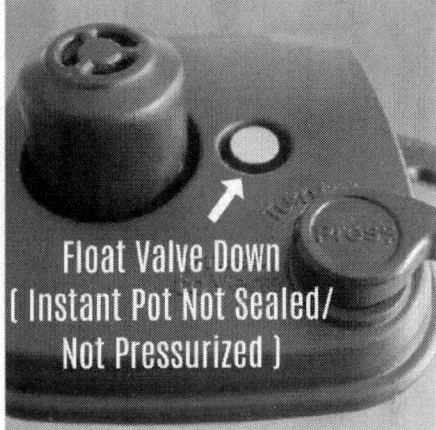

Float Valve Up (Instant Pot Sealed/ Pressurized)

Float Valve Down (Instant Pot Not Sealed/ Not Pressurized)

- When the Instant Pot Ultra is under pressure, the Float Valve goes up and the Instant Pot is sealed. It cannot be opened. Don't try to force it open!
- When the Instant Pot Ultra isn't under pressure, the Float Valve goes back down, and is level with the lid.

There are two ways you can release pressure once the Instant Pot Ultra has finished pressure cooking. The recipe you're following will tell you what method to use.

#49-6 HOW TO QUICK RELEASE INSTANT POT ULTRA

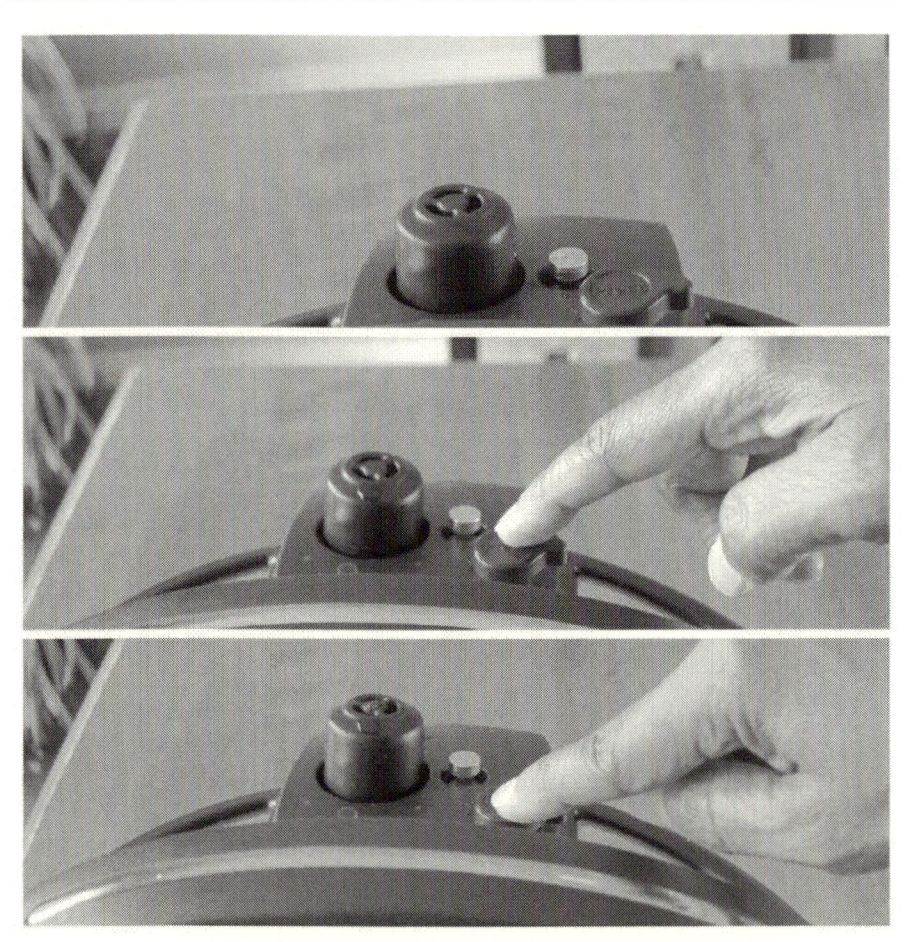

- To do a Quick Release of pressure (QR), press down on the Steam Release Button until it locks into place, and steam begins to come out of the Steam Release Valve.
- ***Be sure your hand is not above the Steam Release Valve while the pressure is being released.***

- The Float Valve will go from the up position to the down position once the Instant Pot Ultra has depressurized and all the steam has been released.
- It is now safe to open the Instant Pot Ultra.

#49-7- HOW TO NATURAL RELEASE (NR) / NATURAL PRESSURE RELEASE (NPR) INSTANT POT ULTRA

- To do an Instant Pot Natural Release of Pressure (NPR), wait for the Float Valve to go down on its own.
- This can take anywhere from 5 minutes to 30 minutes, depending on how much liquid is in the Instant Pot. The more liquid you have, the longer it takes for the Instant Pot to release pressure on it's own.
- If you're in a hurry, you can wait for 15 minutes for the Instant Pot natural release, and then

release the remaining pressure using the quick release method.

#49-8- INSTANT POT ULTRA INITIAL TEST RUN / WATER TEST

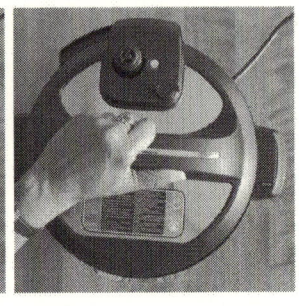

- Attach the power cord to the Instant Pot Ultra, and plug it into an outlet.
- Pour 1 cup water into inner pot. You can add more water, but your Instant Pot will just take longer to come to pressure.
- Close the Lid.

If the display is off, press the knob/dial to turn on the display.

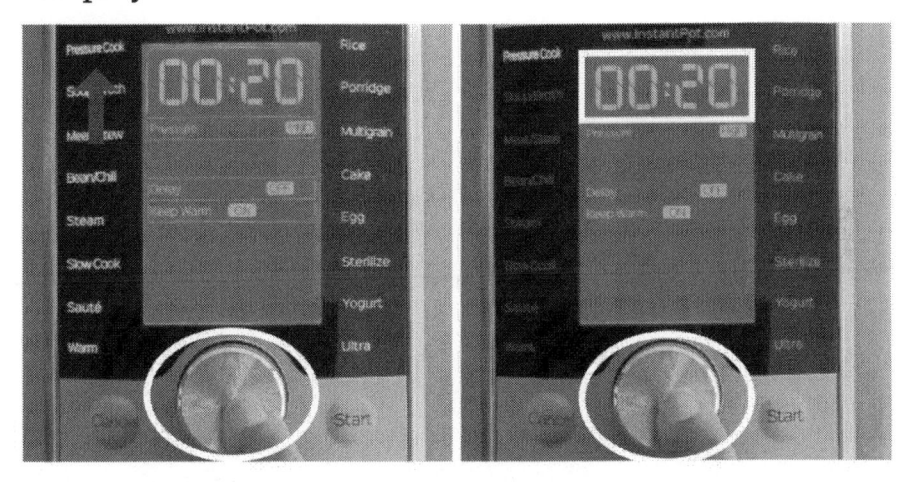

- The 'Pressure Cook' option will be blinking.
- Press the dial to select the 'Pressure Cook' option.
- The cooking time (in my case it's 00:20 i.e. 20 minutes; your display may have a different time) will have a box around it that's blinking.

- Press the dial to select the cooking time.

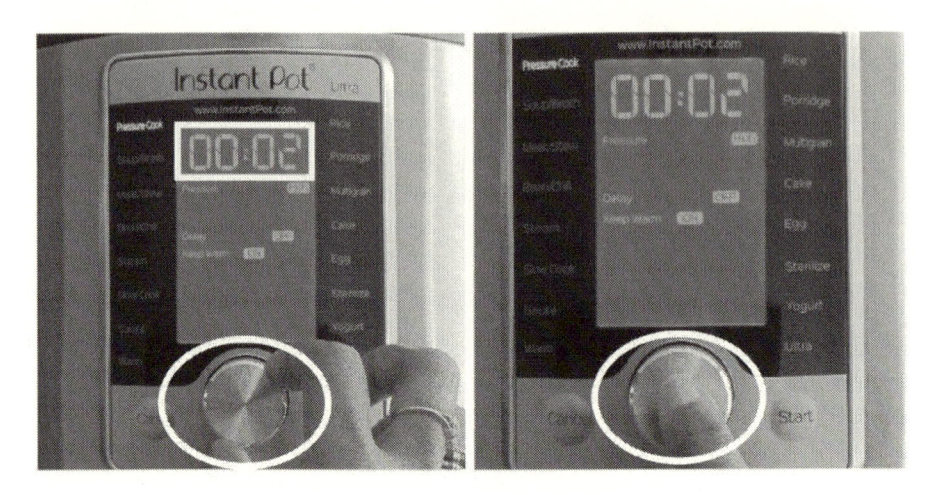

- Now, the time will be blinking.
- Turn the dial until the time changes to 00:02 (2 minutes).
- Press the dial to confirm the time.

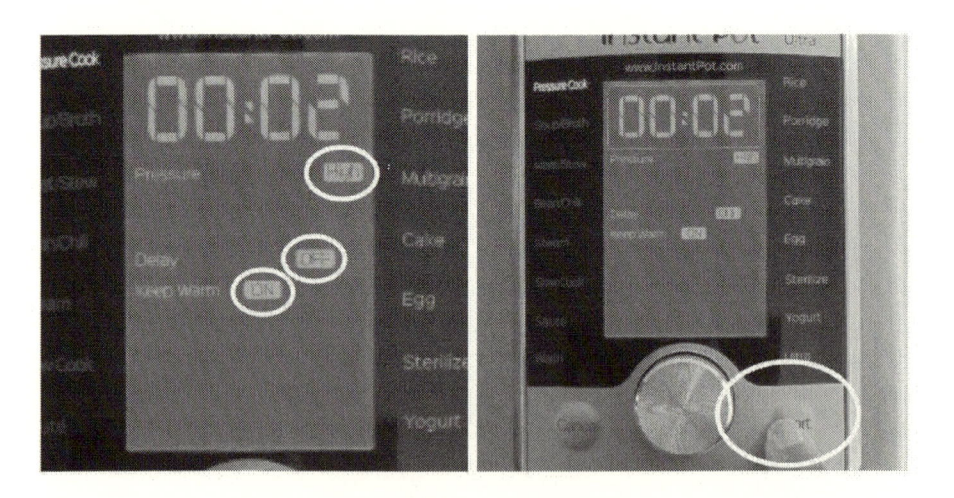

- We'll keep the default settings for Pressure level (High), Delay Start (Off), and Keep Warm mode (On).
- Press Start to begin the pressure cooking.

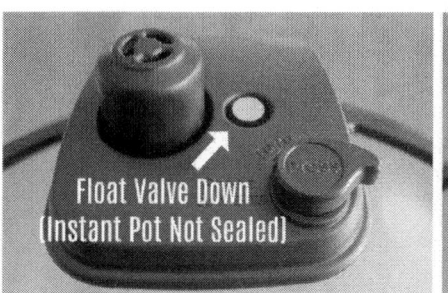

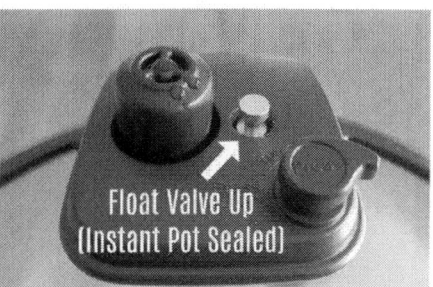

- The Instant Pot Float Valve will go from the down position to the up position once the Instant Pot has sealed. This can take up to 10 minutes for 1 cup of liquid.
- There will be some hissing and steaming, and all sorts of noises coming from the Pressure Release Valve and the Float Valve while the Instant Pot is coming to pressure. There is nothing to worry about!
- You might also notice a plastic-like odor. This can happen during first use, and shouldn't happen again.

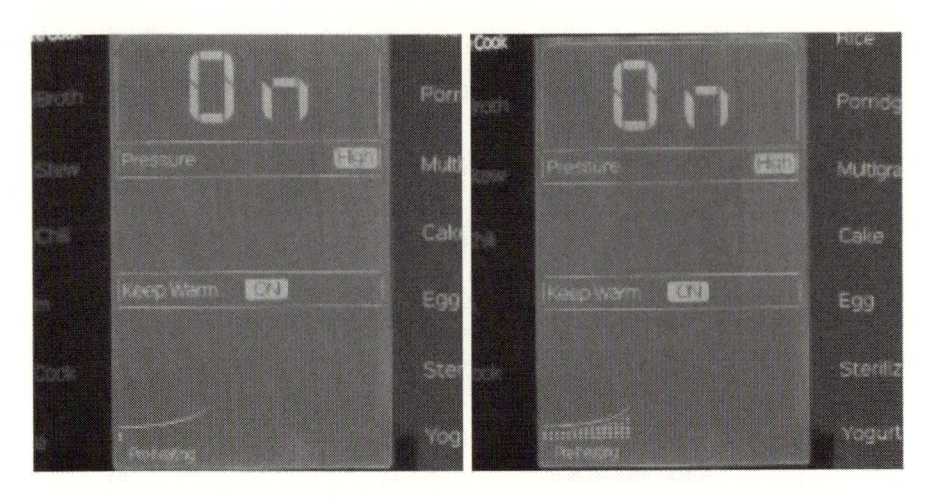

- The display with change to 'On' and will remain 'On' until the Instant Pot reaches pressure.
- Notice that the graph on the bottom of the display will show that the pre-heating is complete.
- The Display will change from 'On' to 2 minutes (00:02) and will count down from 00:02 to 00 00.
- Notice that the graph on the bottom tells you the cooking progress.

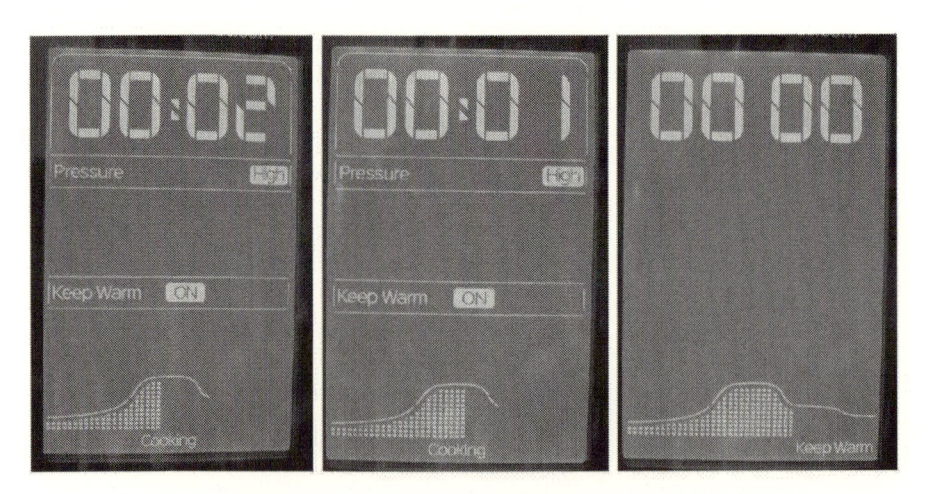

- Once the Instant Pot Ultra is in 'Keep Warm' mode (as seen on bottom right of the display), it will begin to count UP from 00 00.

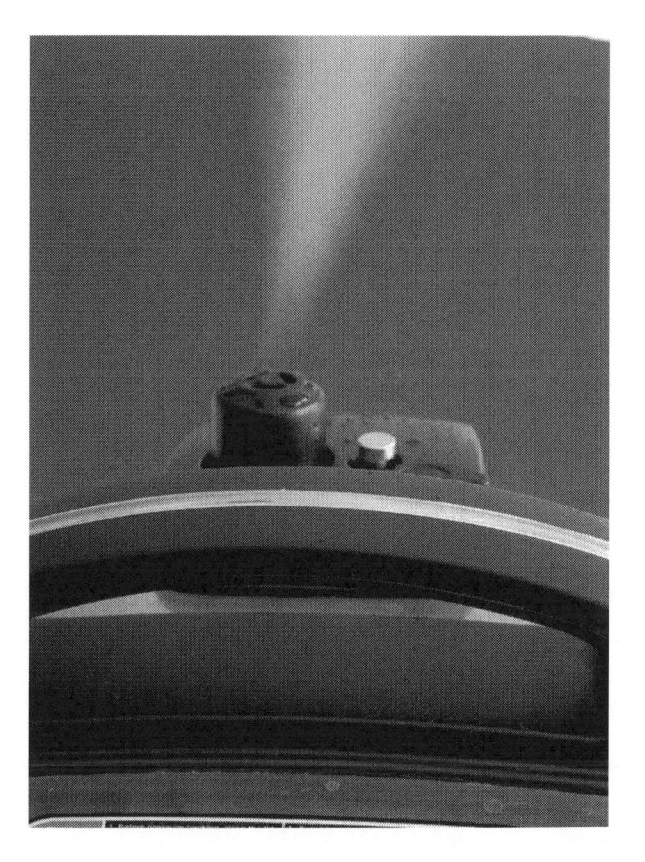

- Do a Quick Release of pressure (QR) as detailed above in the How to Quick Release section.
- Or wait till the pressure releases on it's on as detailed above in the How to Natural Release (NR)/ Natural Pressure Release (NPR) section.

- Press Cancel.
- Open the Instant Pot.
- Initial Test Run is now complete!

Here are the most important differences between the Instant Pot Ultra vs Instant Pot Duo that you need to know about as a beginner:

	Instant Pot DUO	Instant Pot ULTRA
Function Selection	• There are separate buttons for each cooking function. • Use the 'Manual' mode/button to pressure cook.	• Use the knob/dial to toggle between functions and to select options. • Select the 'Pressure Cook' function to pressure cook instead of using a 'Manual' mode.
Pressurizing and Steam Release	• The Steam Release Handle moves between the 'Sealing' and 'Venting' positions. • The Steam Release Handle has to be manually moved to the 'Sealing' position when the Instant Pot is closed.	• The Steam Release Button is pushed down to lock into venting mode and turned counter-clockwise to seal again. • The Steam Release Button automatically resets to the 'Sealing' position when the lid is opened or closed.
Float Valve	• The Float valve is at level of lid when the Instant Pot Duo is sealed and below the level of the lid when it's not sealed.	• The Float valve is above level of lid when the Instant Pot Ultra is sealed and at the level of the lid when it's not sealed.

Now that you've completed the initial test run / water test, you're ready to cook your first dish. I suggest either Instant Pot Rice or Instant Pot Hard Boiled Eggs for your first attempt. But all my recipes are written with beginners in mind and have step-by-step instructions and photographs.

I also strongly recommend that you follow the recipe exactly the first few times – don't substitute ingredients and change quantities. Once you're more comfortable with cooking in your Instant Pot Ultra, you can modify the recipes to suit your needs.

#50 INSTANT POT BURN MESSAGE

Are you seeing an Instant Pot burn message? It's a common problem that many Instant Pot users come across! Find out why you're getting the Instant Pot burn error message, how to avoid the problem in the future, and how to recover from a burn error and salvage your meal.

Lately I've been seeing a trickle of complaints about two of my tried and tested recipes: Instant Pot Penne with

Sausage and Instant Pot Jambalaya. People are asking me why they're getting a *burn* error and what it means when the Instant Pot display says *burn*.

I own two Instant Pots, and I never see the *burn* message. I know other bloggers who are also facing this issue with some of their recipes. Their readers are having issues with rice, pasta, and chili recipes in particular. So I did some digging to find out what's going on.

The Instant Pot has a burn-protection sensor that monitors temperature. According to the Instant Pot website, when a high temperature is detected at the bottom of the inner pot, the burn-protection sensor suspends heating. On prior Instant Pot models the warning '*ovHt*'(overheat) is displayed. This message has been changed to '*burn* 'on newer Instant Pot models.

Some people who own multiple models tell me that they see the Instant Pot *burn* message more frequently on the newer Instant Pots than they do the *ovHt* message on the older Instant Pots. They also say that the newer models seem to be reaching a higher temperature than previous models. Some even notice certain 'hot spots' on the bottom of the inner pot, where food tends to scorch.

Getting the *burn* alert doesn't mean that there's something wrong with your Instant Pot. It just means that your Instant Pot works differently from previous models and so recipes written for older models may not work as written, and you'll need to make a few modifications and follow some tried and tested pressure cooking techniques.

It appears that the burn alert happens more often with the newer 8-quart Instant Pots. Both Instant Pots I own are older model 6 quarts, so I borrowed an older model and newer model 8 quart from a couple of friends. I tested the above-mentioned recipes in both Instant Pots numerous times, and made a few discoveries.

If you're seeing the Instant Pot *burn* message, the following sections tell you why this may be happening, how to avoid it in the future, and how to fix it when it happens to you.

#50-1- COMMON REASONS FOR INSTANT POT *BURN* MESSAGE AND HOW TO AVOID IT

1. Sealing Ring Issues

If your sealing ring is not installed properly or if it's missing, your Instant Pot will leak steam, and that will cause the food at the bottom to scorch and your Instant Pot display will say *burn*.

SOLUTION: You need to make sure that the sealing ring is pushed into the sealing ring rack all the way in and all around. Clean the sealing ring after use and don't forget to put it back in place when you begin pressure cooking. Sealing rings can also get worn out or stretched out over time, requiring replacement.

2. *Steam Release is* venting

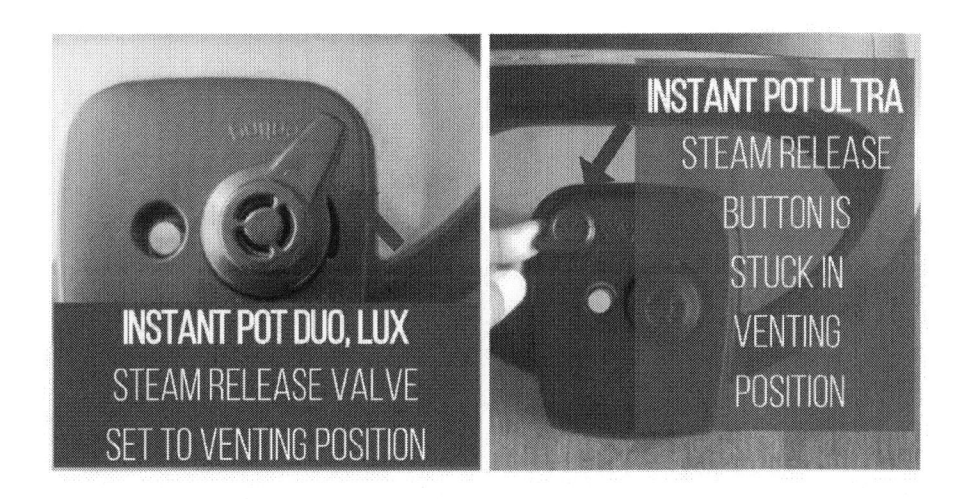

INSTANT POT DUO, LUX STEAM RELEASE VALVE SET TO VENTING POSITION

INSTANT POT ULTRA STEAM RELEASE BUTTON IS STUCK IN VENTING POSITION

If your steam release handle is in the *Venting* position or the steam release button is accidentally stuck in the down position (Ultra model), your Instant Pot will leak steam, and that will cause the contents to burn.

SOLUTION: Verify that the steam release handle or button is in the *Sealing* position.

3. *Not Enough Liquid*

Pressure cookers work by building pressure from steam generated in the pot, which in turn cooks food at high temperatures. This steam cannot be created if there isn't enough liquid in the Instant Pot.

SOLUTION: According to the Instant Pot Company, your Instant Pot pressure cooker requires 2 cups of liquid. If you're just starting out, you can prevent the *burn* notice by always using the minimum recommended quantity of liquid.

Through trial and error, I make recipes with less liquid, even as little as 1/2 cup. To figure out what your minimum quantity of liquid is, you can experiment by doing the water test or initial test run with different quantities of water. According to Jill Nussinow of The Veggie Queen, and author of Vegan under Pressure cookbook, start with 1/4 to 1/2 cup, and increase the quantity with each subsequent test until you're able to get the Instant Pot to come to pressure and stay under pressure for 5 minutes.

Keep in mind that many foods (e.g. vegetables, meats) release liquid and that counts toward the minimum liquid requirement. Canned tomato products and thick sauces don't count toward the quantity of liquid because they are too dense.

Note: When you're adding liquid, make sure it gets underneath any food that's already in the inner pot. This prevents the food from scorching and creates steam.

4. Inner Pot not Deglazed

If you're using the *Sauté* function, food can get stuck on the bottom of the Instant Pot. This can block the heat sensor and trigger the Instant Pot *burn* warning when you start pressure cooking.

SOLUTION: After sautéing and before pressure cooking you need to deglaze the inner pot. Deglazing involves adding a thin liquid like wine, water or broth to the hot surface and scraping the bottom with a silicone scraper or wooden spatula to remove the caramelized and brown bits that are stuck.

Deglazing adds wonderful flavor to your dish, but more importantly, it cleans the inner pot. So any liquid that you add will make full contact with the bottom of the inner pot and that allows the sensor in the Instant Pot to properly register temperature and pressure.

5. Recipe Contains Tomato Products or Prepared Sauces

Recipes containing products like tomato paste, tomato puree, and tomato sauce, cream of chicken, cream of mushroom and Alfredo sauce tend to scorch on the bottom while the Instant Pot is coming to pressure. These ingredients are not thin enough to build steam and some contain fillers like corn starch, flour or cheese which tend to scorch. I see lots of complaints about chili recipes causing the burn notice.

SOLUTION: One pressure cooker technique that's commonly used to prevent foods from burning and sticking to the bottom is to layer the ingredients in the Instant Pot. If the recipe you're using tells you to mix all ingredients together before pressure cooking, but you have issues with the burn error, next time adapt the recipe by doing the following:

- Add the dense and starchy ingredients last: e.g. tomato-based or thick sauces
- Don't stir
- Cover and pressure cook as directed

Another option is to use the Pot-in-Pot (PIP) cooking method to cook dishes that have thick sauces. You don't ever have to worry about the *burn* message when you use the PIP technique.

6. Recipe Contains Starch (Pasta, Rice)

Stirring in and incorporating pasta and rice with all the other ingredients may give you a *burn* message.

SOLUTION: The layering technique described in the above section can also be used for starchy ingredients. Instead of stirring them in, add them at the end, right on top. The pasta or rice needs to be submerged in liquid, so push down on it with a large spoon or spatula to make sure it's covered in liquid.

7. Instant Pot Too Hot After

Sautéing

If you use the *Sauté* function immediately before pressure cooking, especially if you're using high heat, it's possible you'll get an Instant Pot *burn* message.

SOLUTION: Use medium temperature for sautéing and turn off and cool down the Instant Pot after sautéing and deglazing. You can cool it down quicker if you remove the inner pot from the unit and set it on a hot pad or cooling rack.

Alternately, you can sauté on the stovetop and transfer the sautéed food to the Instant Pot to pressure cook.

Note: I find that allowing the Instant Pot to cool down after sautéing is one of the best ways to avoid the burn error.

8. Recipe Tested with Different Instant Pot Size

If the recipe was written for the 6 quart Instant Pot, and you are using an 8 quart, it's possible that there may not be enough liquid for the 8 quart to come to pressure.

SOLUTION: Either double the recipe or add an extra 1/2 to 1 cup of liquid. Keep the cooking time the same.

#50-2- WHAT TO DO WHEN YOU GET AN INSTANT POT BURN MESSAGE

Sometimes the Instant Pot says *'burn'* and then changes to *'On'*. If this happens to you, just say 'thank you' and let it keep cooking. You'll probably have some food stuck on the bottom, but you should be able to salvage most of it.

In some rare cases, the scorched/burnt taste may penetrate the entire dish and you may need to start over. But in most cases, it's possible to salvage your meal when you get the *burn* error, by doing the following:

2. Do a Quick Release of Pressure (QR)

3. Open the Lid

4. If there's nothing stuck to the bottom:

- Let the Instant Pot cool down.
- Most likely, the original liquid may have partially evaporated. Add enough liquid to replace the original liquid that evaporated, plus an additional 1/2 to 1 cup. Lift the food with a spatula to allow the liquid to reach the bottom of the inner pot.
- Resume pressure cooking the dish.

5. If there's food stuck to the bottom:

- Transfer contents that are **not** stuck to the bottom to a separate bowl.
- Scrape and clean out the inner pot so there's nothing stuck on the bottom. *See tip below*
- Allow the Instant Pot unit to cool down.
- Most likely, the original liquid may have fully or partially evaporated. Add enough liquid to replace the original liquid that evaporated, plus an additional 1/2 to 1 cup.
- Resume pressure cooking.

Tip: How to Clean Burnt Food from Inner Pot

- Select *Sauté* mode and allow the Instant Pot to get hot.
- Add 1/2 cup of water to deglaze.
- Scrape the bottom of the inner pot until the food gets unstuck, adding more water as needed.
- Turn off the Instant Pot.

- Empty out the inner pot, wash, and dry.

6. If necessary, reduce the liquid *to desired thickness*

If you added extra liquid to allow the Instant Pot to come to pressure, you might find that the dish is too watery after pressure cooking is complete. In this case, after opening the Instant Pot, select the Sauté function to reduce or cook out the liquid. Another option is to add a mixture of corn starch and cold water to thicken the dish.

#51 INSTANT POT MODELS

Instant Pot Model Details

In the following sections I've detailed all the information I could gather up from the Instant Pot website and try to give you the most pertinent and important information you will need to make a decision about the best Instant Pot size and model to suit your needs.

If a particular model has multiple sizes, I've noted if there are any features that are missing in that particular size of Instant Pot. For example, the Instant Pot LUX model's Mini version does not have the Cake and Multigrain functions, but the 6 quart and 9 quart do have those functions, so I've made a note of that.

My Favorite Picks

I hope I've given you enough information to help you make a decision about which Instant Pot model to buy. If you're still confused about it, I'll share with you my favorite models and why I like them.

The <u>Instant Pot ULTRA 6 Quart 10-in-1</u> is my favorite Instant Pot model. My favorite features are the:

- Auto-seal feature
- Ability to change cooking parameters while it's cooking
- Quick release button
- Cooking progress graph
- Snazzy look

My next favorite Instant Pot model is the <u>Instant Pot DUO80 8 Quart 7-in-1</u>. I like this Instant Pot because:

- It's great for cooking larger amounts of food for a family of my size (5 people).
- You can cook extra portions and have leftovers without overfilling the Instant Pot.

My final choice is the <u>Instant Pot DUO60 6 Quart 7-in-1</u>. This was my first Instant Pot and I still love it because:

- It's just a great value.
- It has all the functionality you would need in an Instant Pot at an affordable price.

10 MOST COMMON INSTANT POT MISTAKES

1. FORGET TO PLACE THE INNER POT BACK INTO INSTANT POT BEFORE POURING IN INGREDIENTS

Mistake: It can be chaotic in the kitchen. We've heard many stories of users accidentally pouring ingredients into the Instant Pot housing without the Inner Pot.

This happens more frequently than we all imagined. *It almost happened to us once.*

Solution: Place a silicone mat, glass lid, or wooden spoon on top of the Instant Pot every time you remove the Inner Pot from the Instant Pot. This helps prevent unnecessary damage to your new kitchen tool!

2. OVERFILL THE INSTANT POT

Mistake: Many new users fill their Instant Pot with food & liquid up to the **Max Line** (*sometimes even a stretch over the Max Line*). This may risk clogging the Venting Knob.

Solution: Be mindful that the Max Line printed on Instant Pot's Inner Pot is **not** intended for Pressure Cooking.

- **For Pressure Cooking:** maximum 2/3 full
- **For Pressure Cooking Food that Expands During Cooking** (such as grains, beans, and dried vegetables): maximum 1/2 full

If you accidentally overfilled the pot, *don't panic.* Just make sure to use **Natural Pressure Release** to stay safe and clean.

3. USE QUICK RELEASE FOR FOAMY FOOD OR WHEN IT IS OVERFILLED

Have you seen pictures of applesauce splattered all over the Instant Pot through the Venting Knob?

Mistake: Many new users are unsure when to use Quick Pressure Release and Natural Pressure Release. There's a chance of splattering if users use Quick Release when cooking foamy food, such as grains or beans.

Solution #1: Use Natural Release for foamy food or when the pot is overfilled.

*But wait...*most pasta recipes call for Quick Release, what should we do?

Solution #2: Release the pressure gradually.

You don't have to turn the Venting Knob all the way to Venting Position to release pressure.

The initial release is usually the strongest. So, release the pressure gradually by turning the venting knob **just a little** with your hand or wooden spoon until you hear a hissing sound. Hold it at that position to release the pressure gradually.

We prefer wearing silicone glove and use our hand for more control.

4. PRESS THE TIMER BUTTON TO SET COOKING TIME

Mistake: Some new users have mistaken the **"Timer" button** for setting the cooking time, then wondered why the Instant Pot is just sitting there not doing anything.

The "Timer" button is actually for **delayed cooking**.

Solution: Before you decide to return your Instant Pot for not working properly, check to see if the "Timer" Button is lit (*the green light shown in photo below*). If so, press **Keep Warm/Cancel Button** to start again.

5. FORGET TO TURN THE VENTING KNOB TO SEALING POSITION

Mistake: It might be a bit overwhelming to use the Instant Pot in the beginning, and it's common to forget to turn the Venting Knob to the Sealing Position when cooking.

Solution: Make it a habit to turn the Venting Knob to Sealing Position <u>every time</u> you start pressure cooking. Don't walk away until you made sure the Floating Valve has popped up.

6. PUT INSTANT POT ON THE STOVETOP AND ACCIDENTALLY TURNED THE DIAL

Mistake: Due to convenience or limited counter space, some users like to place their Instant Pot on the stovetop. Sometimes, things happen...and we see melted burnt Instant Pot bottom.

Sorry, we don't have a picture to show you the aftermath, but we see this happen frequently.

Solution: Please don't put the Instant Pot directly on the stovetop. Some users lay a wooden board between the stovetop and Instant Pot to prevent this disaster.

7.1- COOKING LIQUID: TOO THICK/NOT ENOUGH LIQUID

Mistake: As a new user, it's not intuitive on how much cooking liquid to use. If there's not enough cooking liquid or the liquid is too thick, Instant Pot will not be able to generate enough steam to get up to pressure.

Solutions: Unless stated otherwise in a recipe...

- We recommend new users to use **1 cup of total liquid** until they get comfortable with the machine.
- Always add thickener such as cornstarch, flour, arrowroot, or potato starch **after** the pressure cooking cycle.

7.2- COOKING LIQUID: TOO MUCH LIQUID

Mistake: On the contrary, when there is too much cooking liquid in the Instant Pot, it will increase the overall cooking time (both time to get up to pressure & Natural Release time). This may overcook the food.

Plus, too much cooking liquid will dilute the seasoning, resulting in a bland dish.

Solution: Unless stated in a recipe, we recommend new users to use **1 cup of total liquid** until they get comfortable with the machine.

8. FORGET TO PUT THE SEALING RING BACK IN THE LID BEFORE COOKING

Mistake: Since the silicone sealing ring absorbs the food smell, many users regularly air out/wash the sealing ring. It's easy to forget to place it back into the lid before using the Instant Pot.

If the sealing ring is not properly installed, steam will come out around the edge of the lid and the Instant Pot will not get up to pressure.

Solution: Make it a habit to ensure the sealing ring is properly installed every time, before you close the lid for pressure cooking.

9. USE RICE BUTTON FOR COOKING ALL TYPES OF RICE

Mistake: We've heard some new Instant Pot users have less than satisfactory results with their rice cooked in the Instant Pot using the "Rice" Button.

Don't be discouraged!

Solution: Different types of rice require different **water to rice ratios** & **cooking times**. For best results, we like to use the **"Manual" Button** for most control on Cooking Method & Time.

10. USE HOT LIQUID IN A RECIPE THAT CALLS FOR COLD LIQUID

Mistake: Some users ran into a problem that all their Instant Pot meals were undercooked. We later found that they always start cooking by pouring hot water into the Instant Pot.

Using hot liquid in a recipe that calls for a cold liquid shortens the overall cooking time, because Instant Pot will take a shorter time to come up to pressure.

Since the food starts to cook when Instant Pot is heating up & going up to pressure, and this part of the cooking time is shortened, the food may come out undercooked.

Solution: Use cold liquid to cook or adjust the cooking time stated in the recipe accordingly.

INSTANT POT FREQUENTLY ASKED QUESTIONS

We've gathered some of the most Frequently Asked Questions for Instant Pot below.

If you couldn't find the answer to your question or if you have a great answer to a commonly asked question that's not listed below.

Read Before Purchasing Instant Pot

1. WHAT IS AN INSTANT POT? IS IT THE SAME AS A PRESSURE COOKER?

Instant Pot is a **Third Generation Programmable Electric Pressure Cooker**. In fact, it's currently one of the most popular electric pressure cooker brands!

Besides pressure cooking, you can use the Instant Pot to slow cook, cook rice, brown meat, steam food, keep food warm, and make homemade yogurt!

Comparing to traditional stovetop pressure cookers, Instant Pot gives you the freedom to "set-it-and-forget-it", no more standing by the stove to babysit the pot as it cooks.

Also, instead of using an external heat source (stovetop pressure cooker), Instant Pot uses an internal heat source powered by electricity.

2. INSTANT POT VS. SLOW COOKER?

Slow Cooker (aka Crockpot) heats food at a lower temperature than common cooking methods such as boiling, baking, and frying. Thus, takes longer to cook food.

While Instant Pot, most often used as a pressure cooker, heats food at a higher temperature due to a sealed cooking environment. Thus, cooks faster.

However, as mentioned above, Instant Pot also offers the Slow Cook function. Since we love pressure cooking so much, we rarely use our Instant Pots for slow cooking.

3. WHY IS EVERYONE RAVING ABOUT THEIR INSTANT POTS?

We *love* our dear Instant Pots for many reasons, and here are some of the top reasons:

- **Huge Timesaver** – Cooks most food faster
- **Easy to Use**
- **Safe to Use** – UL & ULC certified with 10 or more built-in safety mechanisms
- **Quiet** – Unlike loud & noisy traditional stovetop pressure cookers
- **Budget-Friendly** – Instant Pot available below $100 USD
- **Hands-Off Cooking** – "set-it-and-forget-it"
- **Can Sauté/Brown Food Directly in the Pot**
- **Yogurt!** Yes – you can make yogurt!

4. IS IT EASY TO COOK WITH AN INSTANT POT?

Yes! There's definitely a learning curve to cook with pressure cookers and Instant Pot, especially if you're new to the method of pressure cooking.

But no worries! Once you get the hang of it, it's relatively easy. Besides, you've got us right here helping you along the way!

5. DOES INSTANT POT REALLY SPEED UP THE COOKING PROCESS?

Cooking in any pressure cooker is almost always faster.

It may not be noticeable for some quick to cook food such as broccoli, eggs or shrimps.

However, tender and juicy pulled pork can be done in under 90 minutes, when it usually takes 2 – 4 hours to make in the oven.

6. ARE THERE ANY DISADVANTAGES WITH COOKING IN INSTANT POT?

One disadvantage of cooking with any pressure cooker is that you can't inspect, taste, or adjust the food along the way.

That's why it's essential, especially in the beginning, to follow tested Instant Pot Recipes with accurate cooking times, seasoning, and amount of liquid to ensure the food quality.

7. IS INSTANT POT SAFE TO USE?

Modern day electric pressure cookers such as the Instant Pot are quiet, very safe and easy to use.

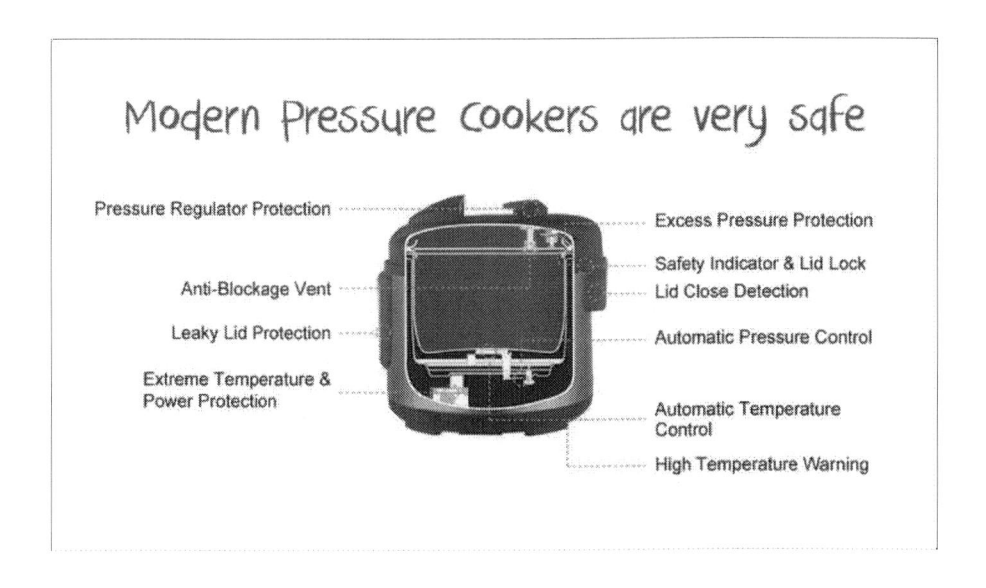

Modern Pressure Cookers are very safe

- Pressure Regulator Protection
- Anti-Blockage Vent
- Leaky Lid Protection
- Extreme Temperature & Power Protection
- Excess Pressure Protection
- Safety Indicator & Lid Lock
- Lid Close Detection
- Automatic Pressure Control
- Automatic Temperature Control
- High Temperature Warning

8. WHAT IS INSTANT POT'S WORKING PRESSURE?

The current Instant Pot models have working pressure in the range of 10.15~11.6 psi.

9. CAN INSTANT POT BE USED FOR PRESSURE CANNING?

This is a direct quote from Instant Pot's official website: "Instant Pot has not been tested for food safety in pressure canning by USDA. Due to the fact that programs in Instant Pot IP-CSG, IP-LUX and IP-DUO series are regulated by a pressure sensor instead of a thermometer, the elevation of your location may affect the actual cooking temperature. For now, we wouldn't recommend using Instant Pot for pressure canning purpose.

10. CAN I USE INSTANT POT FOR PRESSURE FRYING?

Please **don't** attempt to pressure fry in any electric pressure cookers! The splattering oil may melt the gasket.

KFC uses a commercial pressure fryer (modern ones operate at 5 PSI) specially made to fry chickens.

11. WHICH INSTANT POT MAKES YOGURT?

All **Instant Pot DUO, DUO Plus, Ultra Models** have the Programmable Yogurt Function for making Instant Pot Yogurt!

12. WHICH INSTANT POT SHOULD I BUY?

Instant Pot currently offers 4 lines of Instant Pot products:

- LUX Models: LUX Mini 3 Qt 6-in-1, LUX 6 Qt 6-in-1, LUX 8 Qt 6-in-1
- DUO Models: DUO Mini 3 Qt 7-in-1, DUO60 6 Qt 7-in1, DUO80 8 Qt 7-in-1
- DUO Plus Models: DUO Plus 3 Qt 9-in-1, DUO Plus 6 Qt 9-in-1, DUO Plus 8 Qt 9-in-1
- Ultra-Models: Ultra 3 Qt 10-in-1, Ultra 6 Qt 10-in-1, Ultra 8 Qt 10-in-1

Which Instant Pot you should buy highly depends on your budget, cooking needs, the amount of food you normally cook, or how tech-savvy you are?

13. WHICH SIZE SHOULD I BUY?

Instant Pot comes in 3 different sizes: 3 Quart, 6 Quart, and 8 Quart. (Instant Pot Company has discontinued their Instant Pot 5 quart models).

The right Instant Pot Size depends on what type, size, and quantity of food you'll cook with your Instant Pot.

14. WHAT INSTANT POT ACCESSORIES DO I NEED?

Here's our hand-picked list of the most popular Instant Pot Accessories among fellow Instant Pot users

1. Must Have: Silicone Sealing Ring

Every Instant Pot comes with 1 Silicone Sealing Ring. The Sealing Ring is critical to the pressure cooking process, and they do wear and tear over time.

If the ring is damaged or you find that steam starts to leak around the lid, you won't be able to use your Instant Pot until you replace the Instant Pot Sealing Ring with a new one.

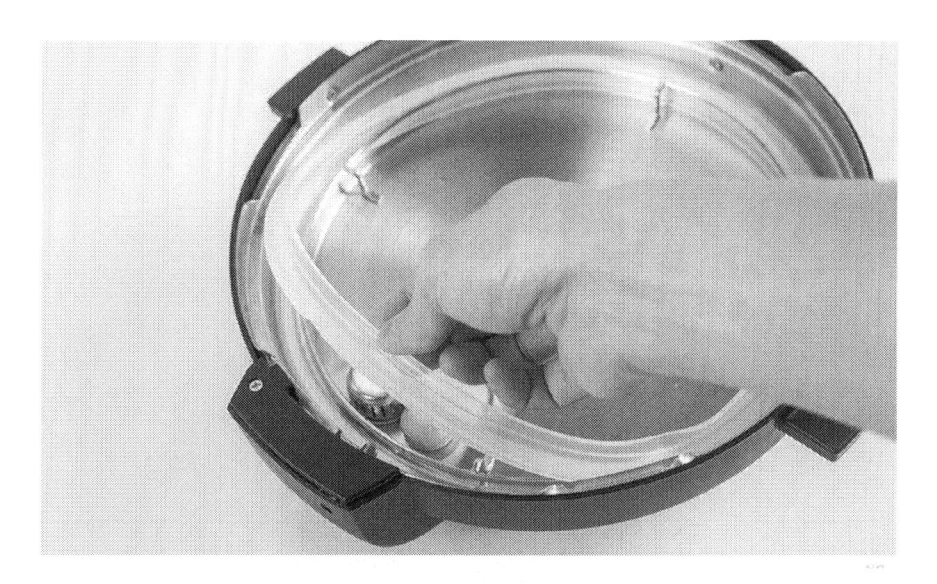

*Pro Tip: Avoid buying sealing rings from third parties, as it is vital to Instant Pot's safety features. Direct Quote from the Instant Pot Company: *"There may be serious safety concerns associated with using an untested sealing ring on Instant Pot products."*

2. Sweet & Savory Silicone Sealing Rings

These Sweet & Savory Silicone Sealing Rings are super handy!

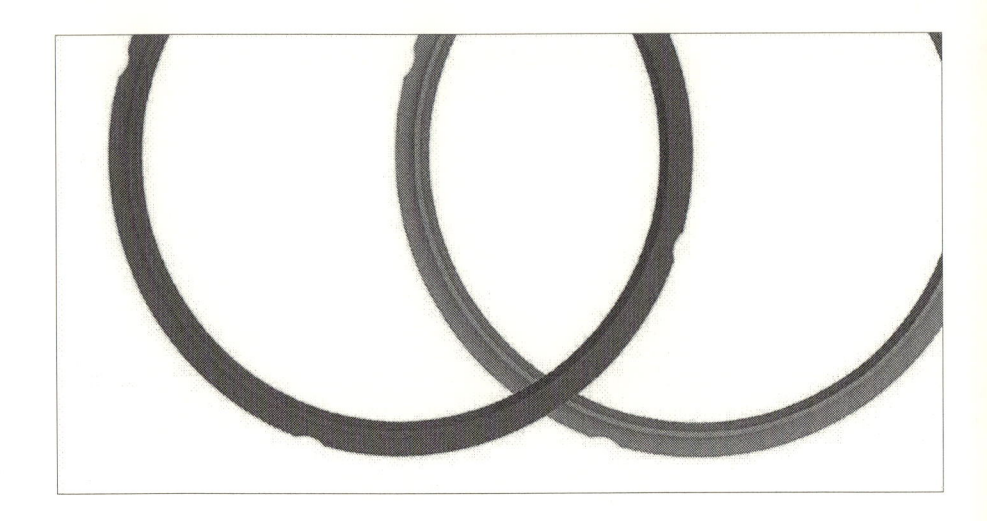

Since the Silicone Sealing Ring tends to absorb the food odor after cooking, many users like to use separate sealing rings for cooking Savory vs. Sweets.

With 2 separate colors, you don't have to worry about mixing them up again!

3. Stainless Steel Inner Pot

Every Instants Pot comes with 1 Stainless Steel Inner Pot.

However, it's often very handy to have an extra Instant Pot Inner Pot. For example, you can use one for cooking and the other for storing leftovers with the glass or silicone lid in the fridge.

4. Non-Stick Inner Pot

This ceramic non-stick inner pot is both PTFE and PFOA free. If you prefer a non-stick inner pot, this is a good option for your 6 quart Instant Pot.

5. Tempered Glass Lid

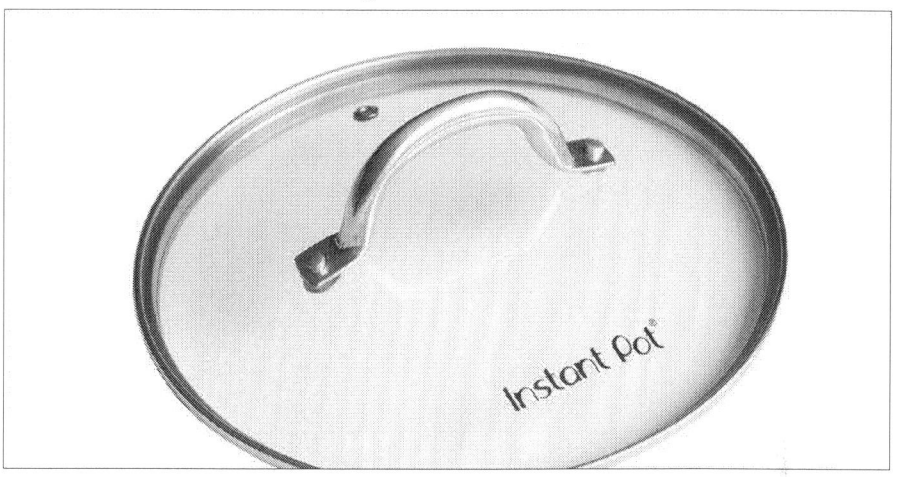

This Glass Lid is great for slow cooking in the Instant Pot. You can use this Instant Pot Glass Lid for "Keep Warm Mode" and storing the whole inner pot with leftovers in the fridge.

*Note: This works with the Slow Cook function on all Instant Pot models purchased after Jan. 2014.

6. Silicone Cover

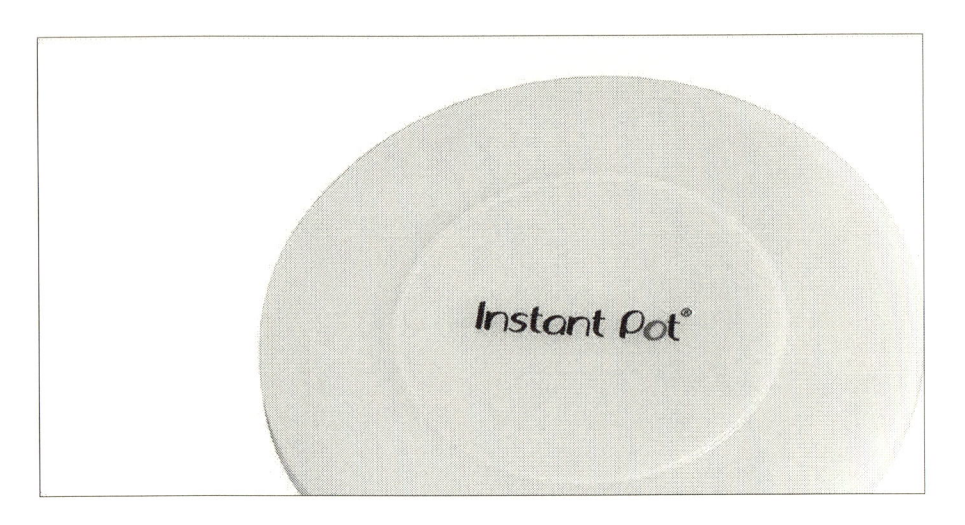

This cover fits your 6 quart Instant Pot's Inner Pot. It's a great way to store leftovers straight in the inner pot without dirtying another container, especially if you don't have the above Instant Pot Glass Lid.

7. Silicone Mitts

These food-grade heat resistant silicone mitts are more flexible than the full-on silicone gloves. It will not provide as much protection, but it is more convenient for lighter work, as you can easily slip them on and off.

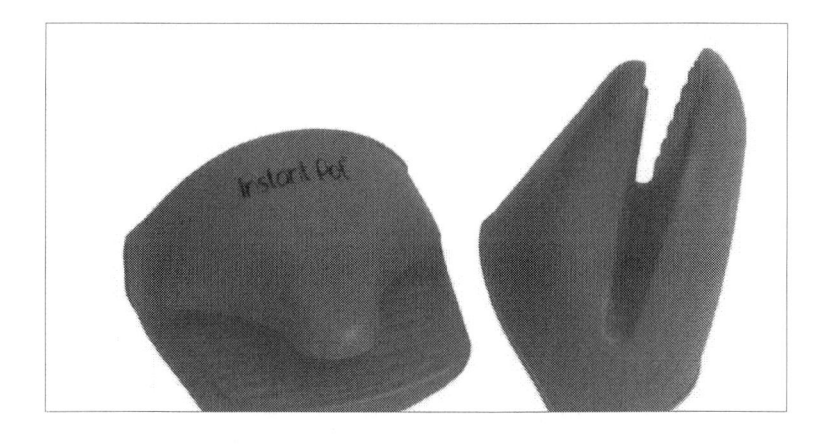

Plus, it'll bring out your inner child with some puppet fun!

Instant Pot Inserts
8. Must Have: 100% Premium Stainless Steel Steamer Basket

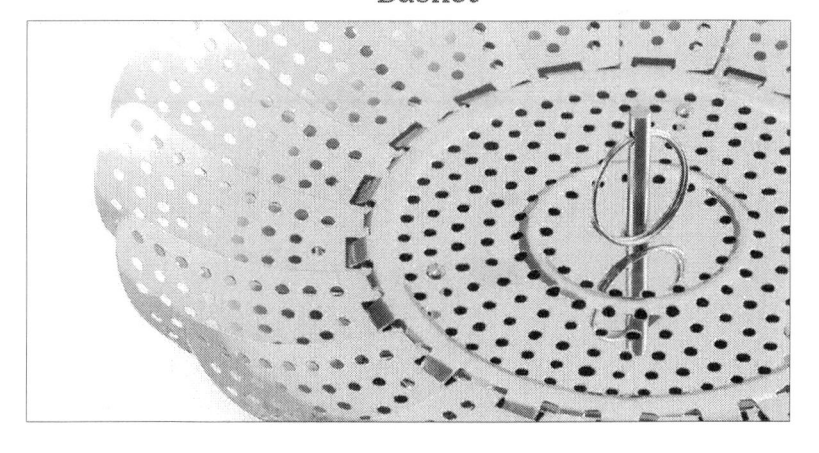

Another great steamer basket we use frequently! Fits perfectly in the Instant Pot. The feet can keep the veggies and other food out of the liquid for optimal steaming results in your Instant Pot.

9. Must Have: Stainless Steel Steaming Rack Stand (5 inch Diameter)

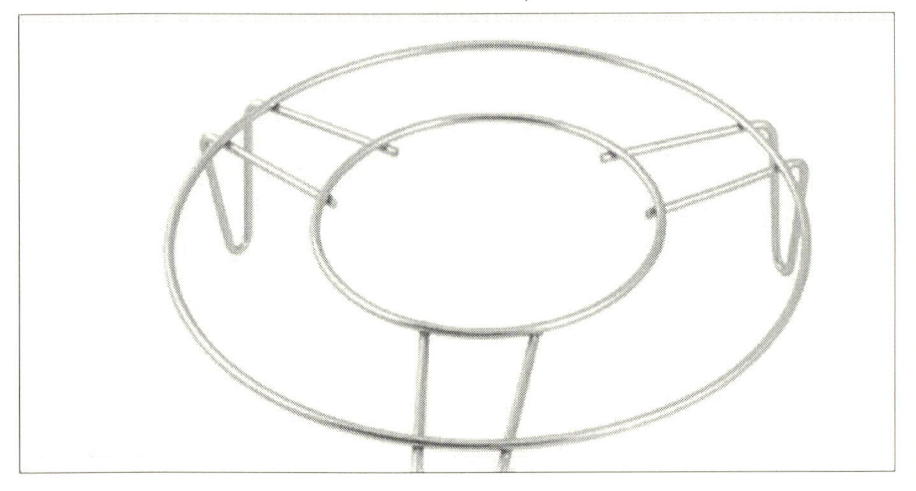

A popular budget-friendly steaming rack we couldn't live without! They're so useful that we actually have 4 *of these* for daily usage.

It's especially useful for our Pot-In-Pot (PIP) Recipes such as Instant Pot Teriyaki Chicken and Rice and regular steaming on stovetop.

10. Stackable Stainless Steel Steamer Insert Pans

ekovana Stackable Stainless Steel Pressure Cooker Steamer Insert Pans - For Instant Pot...

- VERSATILE - 2 tier stackable pans allowing for variety of foods to be cooked...
- HEALTHY & CONVENIENT - Skip the microwave ovens and reheat leftover food or curry in your...

These stainless steel stackable steamer pans are popular among Instant Pot users and they are just perfect for the Pot-in-Pot (PIP) cooking method.

11. Wide Rim Mesh Basket

This Steamer Basket is such a game changer!

You can use this as a steamer basket or strainer – wash your vegetables, put them in the basket, and put the basket straight into Instant Pot's inner pot.

It saves time especially when you're making things like chicken stock. You can easily remove all the ingredients at once instead of scooping them out bit by bit.

No wonder this is one of the fans' favorite Instant Pot Accessories!

Note: You'll need to remove the two handles with a plier to fit this basket in Instant Pot.

*Pro Tip: If you don't want to bother with removing the handles, This **Hatrigo Steamer Basket comes** highly recommended as well.

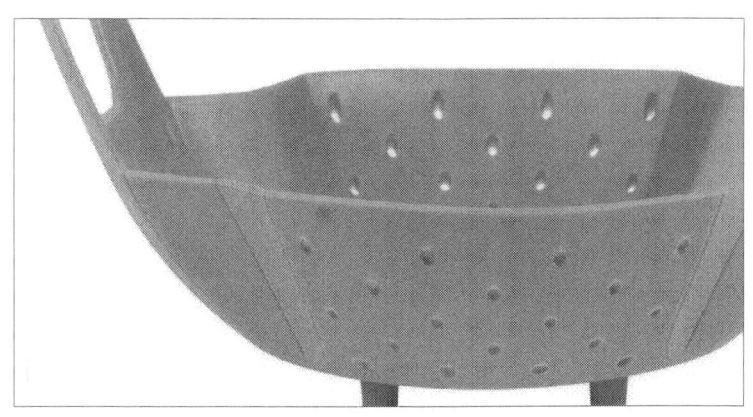

12. Silicone Steamer Basket

This is another popular steamer basket option if you prefer silicone over stainless steel. It's made of BPA free silicone, flexible, easy to clean, with nice long handles, and easy storage.

13. 2 Tiers Bamboo Steamer (8 Inches)

This Bamboo Steamer works great in Instant Pot!

It's the perfect companion for dim sum such as Shumai (Shrimp & Pork Dumplings) or Har Gow (Shrimp Dumplings). Trust me, dim sum simply tastes better in a bamboo steamer as some of its natural
bamboo fragrance will be infused while steaming.

You can use this for steaming veggies too.

For Making Instant Pot Cheesecake
14. 7 Inch Cheesecake Pan with Removable Bottom

This is one of the most popular Instant Pot Accessories cheesecake pans in the Instant Pot community. Make sure to get the 7-inch, as the 8-inch cheesecake pan will not fit in the 6 quart Instant Pot.

For Making Instant Pot Yogurt
15. Euro Cuisine GY60 Greek Yogurt Maker

This BPA free strainer will transfer your homemade Instant Pot yogurt into a thick, creamy Greek yogurt.

Euro Cuisine GY60 Greek Yogurt Maker (shown in below photo) features a stainless steel strainer.

Instant Pot Starter Kit

16. Instant Perrrt! Silicone Starter Kit

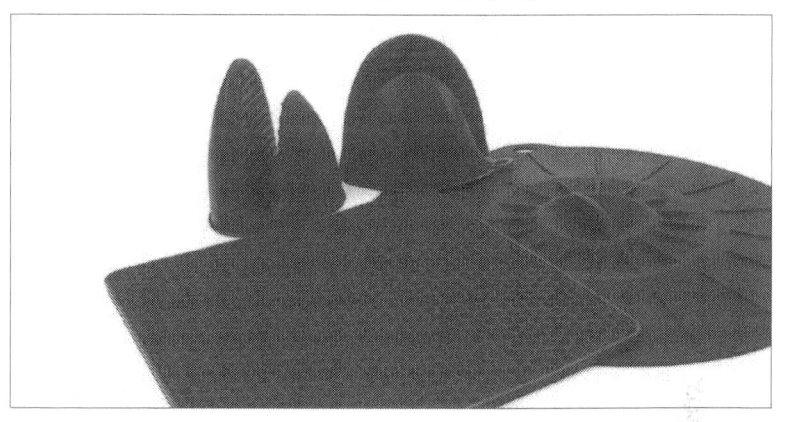

This is a highly popular starter kit among our Instant Pot readers.

This Instant Pot Starter Accessories Kit includes:

- **Pair of Mini Mitts** – Great for gripping the inner pot while sautéing or grabbing the inner pot when removing it from the main unit.
- **Heat Resistant Mat / Pot Holder** – Keep your counters & tables safe by sitting your inner pot on these heat resistant pot holders.
- **Suction Sealing Lid** – Cover the inner pot with this lid to keep the heat in your pot when it's removed from the main unit. Or you can put it over the main unit while your inner pot is removed, so you won't accidentally pour ingredients into your main unit (*this happens more easily and often than you'd think*!?).

Handling Hot Containers
17. Hot Dish Retriever Tongs

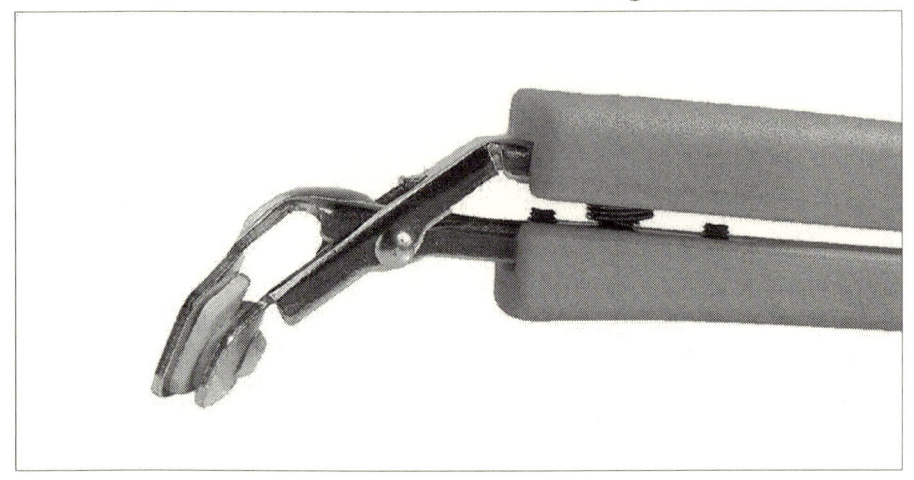

Great for taking hot pans and dishes out of the Instant Pot for the Pot-in-Pot (PIP) cooking method.

18. Eco Grab Heat Resistant Silicone Gloves

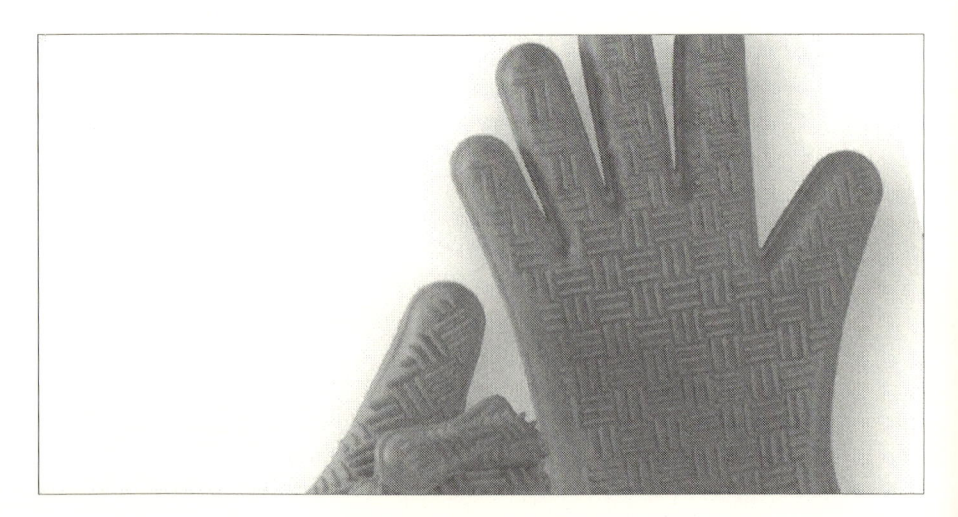

We always suffer with wet oven mitts. Never ever grab a hot pan with wet oven mitts as the heat transfers so much faster this way!

So, we bought these quality, well-made Heat Resistant Silicone Gloves. They are waterproof and steam cannot penetrate through. This Best Seller is made with premium FDA rated silicone.

What do you think of these Instant Pot Accessories?

Have fun with your Instant Pot Pressure Cooker!

15. WHAT ACCESSORIES OR CONTAINERS CAN I USE IN INSTANT POT?

You can use any oven-safe accessories and containers.

Take note that different materials will conduct heat differently, so cooking times may vary when you use different containers.

We recommend using stainless steel containers as they conduct heat quickly.

16. I JUST GOT MY INSTANT POT. WHAT SHOULD I DO FIRST?

Congratulations and welcome to the Instant Pot Tribe!

Time to overcome your fear and unbox your Instant Pot! Here's a Step-by-Step Guide: **Instant Pot Setup**

Then, you should conduct a Water Test with your brand new Instant Pot!

17. WHAT IS THE WATER TEST?

It's simply running a test run before you start experimenting with food. It also allows you to get a feel of how the pressure cooker works (i.e. which buttons to use, how to do quick release).

18. I'M CONFUSED WITH ALL THE INSTANT POT TERMS AND ACRONYMS.

Ready to learn the Instant Pot Codes?

Instants Pot Acronyms

1. IP, Instapot, Magic Pot, Pot = Instant Pot

2. Pothead, Potters = Instant Pot users

3. PC = Pressure Cooker

- A pressure cooker is a tightly sealed cooking pot that cooks food with high pressure.

4. EPC = Electric Pressure Cooker

- Instant Pot is one of many brands of Electric Pressure Cookers in the market.

5. HP = High Pressure

- High Pressure is the pressure cooking mode that cooks at 10.2 – 11.6 psi.

6. LP = Low Pressure

- Low Pressure is the pressure cooking mode that cooks at 5.8 – 7.2 psi.

7. NR, NPR = Natural Release or Natural Pressure Release

After the cooking cycle finished, let the Instant Pot releases the pressure on its own (let it sit) until the Floating Valve (metal pin) completely drops.

8. QR, QPR = Quick Release or Quick Pressure Release

After the cooking cycle finished, move the Venting Knob from Sealing Position to Venting Position to quickly release the pressure inside the pressure cooker. Wait until the Floating Valve (metal pin) completely drops before opening the lid.

9. HA = High Altitude

Your current location's altitude affects the optimal pressure cooking time. So, if you live in a high altitude city over 3000 ft. above sea level, adjust the cooking times for our recipes using the Pressure Cooker High Altitude Cooking Time Chart.

PRESSURE COOKER HIGH ALTITUDE
Cooking Time Adjustments

ALTITUDE	COOKING TIME
3000 ft	+ 5%
4000 ft	+ 10%
5000 ft	+ 15%
6000 ft	+ 20%
7000 ft	+ 25%
8000 ft	+ 30%
9000 ft	+ 35%
10000 ft	+ 40%
11000 ft	+ 45%
12000 ft	+ 50%

10. PIP = Pot in Pot or Pan in Pot

The Pot-in-Pot method allows you to cook more than 1 dish separately in the same pot at the same time.

You can do this by placing the ingredients in an oven-safe container on a rack inside the pressure cooker, separating it from the liquid and/or ingredients directly in the pot.

For example, you can cook rice and main dish at the same time in the Instant Pot!

11. 5-5-5 = High Pressure 5 minutes, Natural Release 5 minutes, Ice Bath 5 minutes

This is one of the many methods for making Hard Boiled Eggs in the Instant Pot. Same idea with 6-6-6 or 4-4-4.

INSTANT POT TERMINOLOGY

1. Instant Pot LUX, DUO, DUO plus, Ultra, Smart

The Instant Pot Company currently manufactures 5 different product lines of Instant Pot Electric Pressure Cookers: LUX, DUO, and DUO Plus, Ultra, and Smart.

They vary in features, functionalities, designs, sizes, and price.

2. Exterior Pot / Exterior Housing / Cooker Base

The exterior pot or housing refers to the outer brushed stainless steel part – where you place the inner pot.

*Caution: never immerse the exterior Instant Pot housing in any type of liquid.

3. Inner Pot / Insert / Liner / Stainless Steel Inner Pot

The inner pot is the removable 3-ply bottom stainless steel cooking pot (as shown in photo below) – where you place your food/liquid.

*Note: it's dishwasher safe.

Each Instant Pot Electric Pressure Cooker comes with 1 stainless steel inner pot. You can purchase an extra one for more flexibility:

4. Instant Pot Lid

The few critical parts you need to know about the Instant Pot Lid: Silicone Sealing Ring, Venting Knob, Floating Valve, and Anti-Block Shield (further explained below).

You can also purchase an Instant Pot Glass Lid (for slow cooking, keep warm mode), or Instant Pot Silicone Cover (for storing leftovers in the fridge).

5. Instant Pot Seal / Ring / Sealing Ring / Gasket

The Silicone Sealing Ring is critical to the pressure cooking process. So, it's important to always check if it's seated properly or damaged before you close the lid.

*Note: the silicone ring is dishwasher safe.

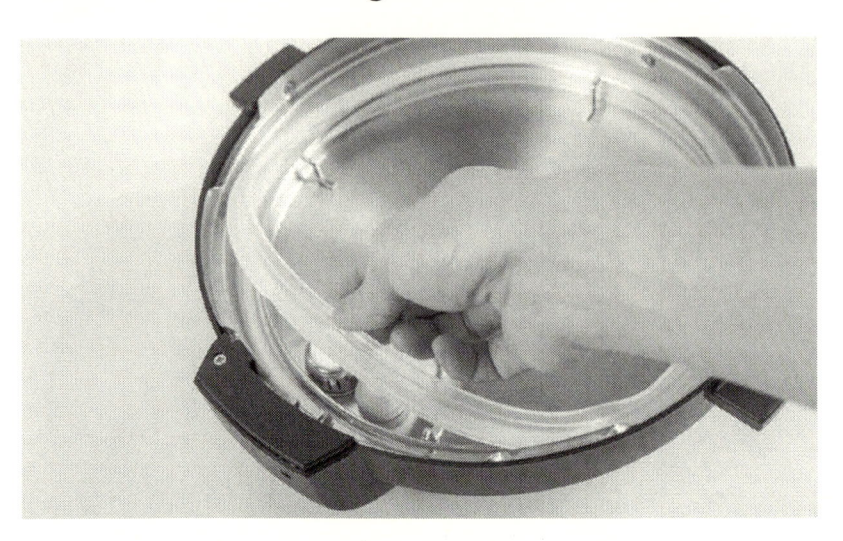

*Pro Tip: It's always good to have spare Silicone Sealing Rings as they do wear and tear over time.

6. Knob / Venting Knob / Steam Release Valve / Pressure Release Handle

It's perfectly normal for the Venting Knob to be loose. You can pull it straight out for washing if necessary.

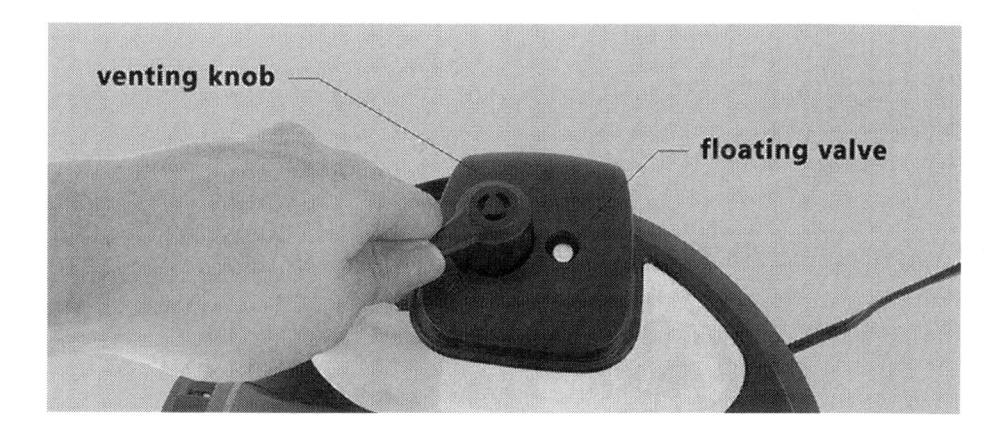

7. Valve / Floating Valve / Pin / Metal Pin

This Floating Valve shows you a key signal whether your Instant Pot has built enough pressure (up to pressure) or has finished releasing pressure (depressurize).

***Note:** different Instant Pot models' Floating Valve may look different than the one shown in photo below

8. Sealing Position / Venting Position

It's critical to ensure the Venting Knob is in the right position for the pressure cooking to go as intended.

- **Sealing Position:** allows you to trap the steam in the pressure cooker (build up pressure)
- **Venting Position:** allows you to release the steam inside the pressure cooker (depressurize)

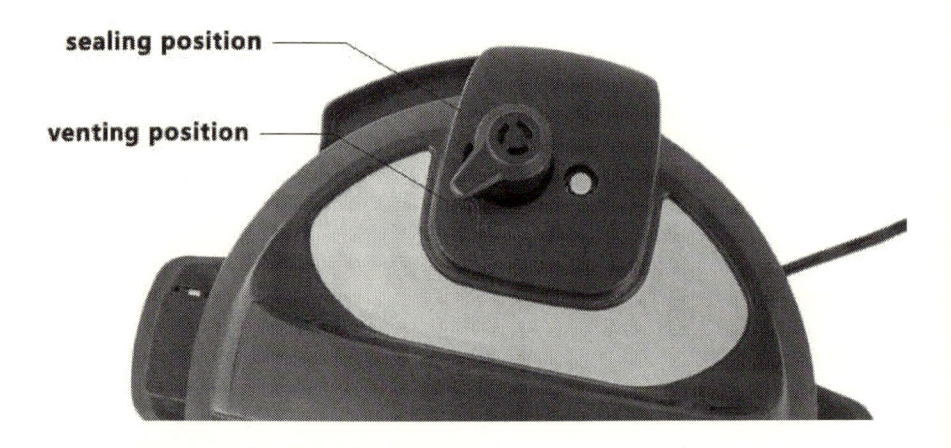

9. Shield / Anti-Block Shield

The Anti-Block Shield is one of the ten safety mechanisms of the Instant Pot that prevents food from interfering with the Venting Knob.

For cleaning, you can push it on the side to lift it up (as shown in photo below), and press it down in position to install it back in.

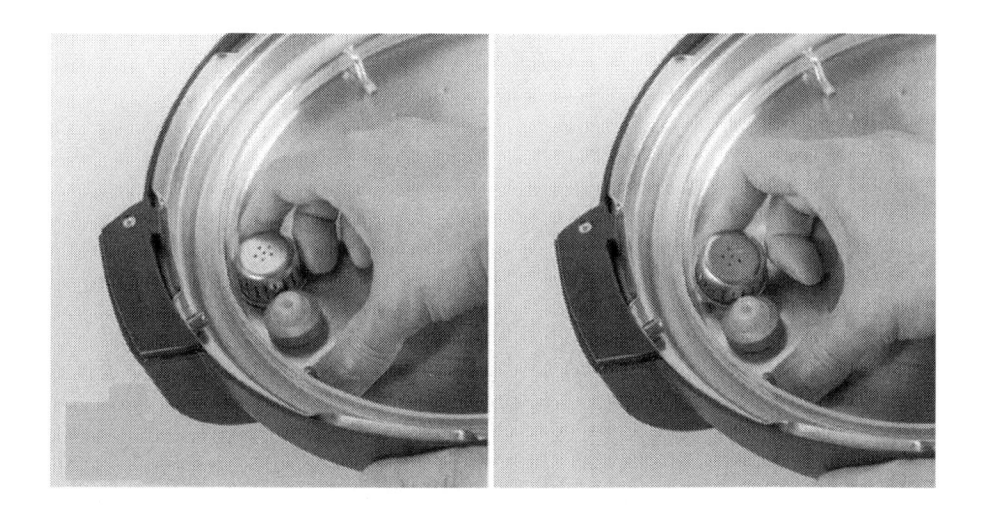

10. Condensation Collector

The flat little plastic cup that comes with your Instant Pot helps collect the condensation that sometimes drip into the gap as you open the Instant Pot Lid.

How to Install the Condensation Collector? First find the slot at the back of Instant Pot, then slide it right in (as shown in photo above).

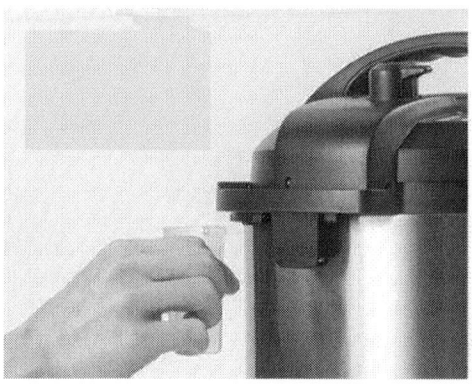

11. Trivet / Rack / Steamer Basket / Steamer Rack

What is a Trivet? It's the stainless steel rack that comes with the Instant Pot! A handy tool for cooking in the Instant Pot – especially great for steaming and Pot-in-Pot.

*Note: each Instant Pot Electric Pressure Cooker should come with a trivet, but they may look slightly different than the one above.

12. Water Test / Initial Test Run

What's the Water Test that everybody talks about?
Some rite of passage into the Pothead Cult?

Ha! This is a recommended step that helps you familiarize yourself with how the Instant Pot Pressure

Cooker works, and makes sure everything is working properly.

If your Instant Pot worked perfectly without conducting the Water Test, don't worry about it.

THANK YOU

I hope these Instant Pot tips and FAQs have answered some of the questions you may have about the Instant Pot.

Thank you for being one of my most loyal clients over the years. It has been my pleasure helping. I am working on building my online presence on the web and as part of this, I am looking to my clients to share an online testimonial.

Would you be willing to take ten minutes to provide me a review on Amazon?

This will allow those that search for me to understand the value I bring to my clients and allow me to stand out in search engine results.

If you are willing (big thank you!).

Thank you so much for taking the time to provide us feedback and review. This feedback is appreciated and very helpful to us.

Best regards,

Rahmouni. K

Made in the
USA
Monee, IL